LEGAL
COUNSEL

NATIONAL LIBRARY OF CANADA CATALOGUING IN PUBLICATION DATA

Vandor, Les
Legal counsel: frequently asked questions about the law

Contents: bk. 1. An introduction to the legal system, individual rights and employ-
ment rights bk. 2. Property rights, family and divorce and company rights bk. 3.
Retirement, representation and wills.

ISBN 1-55022-483-2 V.1.   ISBN 1-55022-485-9 V.2.   ISBN 1-55022-486-7 V.3.

1. Law Canada – Popular works. 1. Title.

KE447.V35 2001   349.71   C2001-900823-7

Author photo on back cover by Marilyn Mikkelsen
Cover and text design by Tania Craan
Layout by Wiesia Kolasinska

Printed by AGMV

Distributed in Canada by
General Distribution Services,
325 Humber College Blvd.,
Toronto, ON M9W 7C3

Published by ECW PRESS
2120 Queen Street East, Suite 200
Toronto, ON M4E 1E2
ecwpress.com

This book is set in Bembo and Futura.

PRINTED AND BOUND IN CANADA

The publication of *Legal Counsel* has been generously supported by the
Government of Canada through the Book Publishing
Industry Development Program. Canadä

Disclaimer: The questions and answers that follow are meant as a guide.
You are encouraged to consult with your own legal practitioner for
details as to your particular situation.

LEGAL COUNSEL

FREQUENTLY ASKED QUESTIONS ABOUT THE LAW

BOOK TWO

Property Rights, Family and Divorce, and
Company Rights

LES VANDOR, QC

ECW PRESS

To my wife of 26 years, Josée

TABLE OF CONTENTS

CHAPTER TWO — FAMILY AND DIVORCE

INTRODUCTION

PARENTAL RESPONSIBILITY: registering children, responsibility for actions of children, power of attorney, elderly family members, marriage and names

NAME CHANGES: legal names, birth certificates, remarriage and names

MISTAKEN IDENTITY: debts

DIVORCE: obtaining a divorce, disclosure of assets, excerpts from divorce act, breakdown of marriage, separation, real estate division, equalization of assets

SUPPORT: pensions, support orders in other provinces, support orders, changes, child support

CUSTODY: joint custody, changes in custody, education, disciplining children

SEPARATION: separation agreement, review, changing financial circumstances, maiden names, marriage contracts, responsibility for debts upon separation

SAMPLE MARRIAGE CONTRACT

CHAPTER THREE — COMPANY RIGHTS

INTRODUCTION

OWNERSHIP: share certificate, common share, preferred share, passing on shares

PARTNERSHIPS: ownership of property, intellectual property, hiding assets, Statute of Elizabeth

PUBLIC AND PRIVATE COMPANIES: public company, private company, trust

LIABILITY: manufacturer's liability, financing a business

DISPUTES: oppression remedy, application to court re oppression, powers of court, business partnerships

PATENT AND TRADEMARK: patents, domain names, the Internet

TRUSTS: spousal

MISCELLANEOUS MATTERS: sex and the law, sex in the workplace, failure to pay rent, seizure of assets

SAMPLE SHAREHOLDER'S AGREEMENT

SAMPLE GENERAL CONTRACT

SAMPLE GENERAL NONDISCLOSURE AGREEMENT

Foreword

by the former Chief Justice of British Columbia

I was pleased when my longtime friend Les Vandor, QC, asked me to write a foreword to the Legal Counsel series of books he has written answering the most often asked questions about the law. This is a project that needs a lot of attention, and I applaud every attempt to explain and clarify the law.

It is often said, incorrectly I believe, that the law is a mystery to most people. That is because everything we do not understand is a mystery to us. The law can be very straightforward, as in the formation of a contract or the definition of negligence, or exceedingly difficult, as in the defence of insanity in a criminal law context or the interpretation of some sections of the Income Tax Act. What makes the difference, of course, is information.

Thus, the most junior lawyer knows that a contract is formed when an offer is accepted; that negligence is doing what a reasonable person would not do or not doing what a reasonable person would do; that the defence of insanity is more difficult and that even lawyers need to look at the most recent decision of the Supreme Court of Canada, *R. v. Stone*, to understand this particular defence; and, as some lawyers say, that only God knows what some sections of the Income Tax Act mean.

So those who wonder about a legal question are searching for information that will help them to answer their questions or to understand that the complexities of some laws — usually dictated by the complexities of society — require much study and research before some questions can be answered.

What is often not understood is that when persons disagree about any matter, legal or otherwise, they are probably operating from different databases. I often think that, if only the public knew what I know about a case, it would agree with my decisions much more readily than is sometimes the case and vice versa in some cases. So it is important for the judiciary and the legal profession to provide information to the public so that it can more readily understand why the law is the way it is and why cases are decided the way they are.

Great strides have been made recently in this direction. Most courts now publish all their decisions on the Internet. Some authors are writing books about the law in engaging and understandable terms. I have tried to explain the judiciary and the criminal law in a legal compendium I have published on the Internet, and Les Vandor has tried to make the law more understandable through the medium of his radio show.

He has now gone one step further in agreeing to write three books about the law. I am happy to have this opportunity to congratulate him for his energy and industry. I am confident that his endeavours will add greatly to public understanding of the law.

The Hon. Allan McEachern
former Chief Justice of British Columbia

Foreword

by the former Chief Justice of Nova Scotia

This book deals with many of the problems that confront and confound all of us in our daily lives whether it be on a personal, family or business level.

Owning a home is the goal of most Canadian families. Acquiring a house appears to be a relatively simple proposition. But houses sit on land, and therein arise some of the most complex problems people face, especially if adequate investigation and care have not been taken before the contract to purchase is signed. Those who buy or rent a condominium or duplex or apartment often wish, after the event, they were forewarned of pending pitfalls.

Consider the family cottage. Parents, convinced that there will never be dissension among their children, who "love the cottage," would be shocked after their demise to find that war has broken out among their offspring. On occasion, ownership and control of the beloved cottage become so fractured that it ends up being sold for the nonpayment of property taxes.

Unfortunately, many families are confronted with differences that lead to separation and divorce. Such circumstances are fraught with myriad difficult issues over who will own property and how the custody of children will be settled. It is much easier for judges to decide who should get Aunt Jessie's vase than how the children will be supported and by whom they will be raised.

None of us needs to establish a large company with its shares traded on a stock exchange to become involved in a corporate or commercial venture that can make us rich or do us in. Often a good idea is worth being patented or developed into a small business. Working with a friend or colleague may lead to the suggestion that a partnership be formed. The implications that result from totally innocent business associations can be devastating if plans are not properly documented.

The one thing that makes this book so useful is that in it Les Vandor, QC, has collected the real life experiences of Canadians. While it is not designed to be a legal text, it offers a practical guide to problems and their solutions.

For all of this, we owe Les Vandor our thanks.

The Hon. Lorne Clarke, OC, QC
former Chief Justice of Nova Scotia

Preface

People write books for many reasons. Some write for money, while others have stories to tell. Some write to fill personal or social needs. I wrote as a result of a number of factors that seemed to coalesce at one time.

The first factor was a client who didn't pay me. I thought at the time that the advice I had given was good. Since I had done the research for the opinion, why not put the information I had gleaned from various sources to good use? I approached the CBC and suggested a call-in show on the topic I had researched. That was in 1992. Thus began for me a stint on radio giving free legal advice. I must thank the CBC (and in particular Dave Stephens and Elizabeth Hay) and its many listeners, whose questions are in this book.

The second factor was a neighbour who lived up the street. We have a variety of people who live nearby. We have economists, physicians, businesspeople, consultants, and military personnel. We have street parties. At a recent party, a neighbour in the book-publishing business suggested I write a book. I said maybe since he was the host and I was a polite guest. Were we under the influence of good cheer, or was this a serious option? I'd get back to him.

The third factor was a propensity to write. I scribbled on various pieces of paper and was fortunate to have had two pieces published in the *Globe and Mail*. I had always dreamed of writing a book of short stories. Law was not on the list. Yet law afforded me the opportunity to write.

In the weeks that followed, I was preoccupied with my ailing father. In the hospital, I engaged in small talk. I suggested a book, and my father said yes. I went home and began to write.

My aim in writing was to increase the public's basic understanding of the law. I didn't need to write just to see my name in print. My clients gave me that in some of the high-profile cases I had the honour of handling. These cases ranged from suing a TV station (the media loved that one) to fighting Revenue Canada (the public loved that one). I hope I have met the goal of public education.

I would like to thank my father and Robert Ferguson (my neighbour). My wife and children took this project in stride, what with all the other crazy things I do. I thank my assistant, Robyn-Erin, for retyping various drafts and reminding me of some of the clients who walked in off the street. Without them, there would be no book. Let me also thank Dallas Harrison, my editor, who fixed my sentence structure. I wish that I could use his talents in my legal drafting. Thank you to all.

Introduction

The law is not a big, scary, incomprehensible beast. Dick the Butcher (an associate of Jack Cade), not Shakespeare, would have killed all lawyers, but lawyers and the law are part of our society, where rules and regulations govern our daily lives.

In primitive societies, the leader of a group or tribal chief would make decisions on a daily basis to settle disputes and set priorities. As a society evolved, the lord of the manor, and ultimately the king or queen, would establish rules and regulations for the orderly conduct of daily affairs. When problems arose, he or she would render a decision. Often the aggrieved persons would be so emotionally caught up with the problem that they would have a friend or family member assist them in advancing their cases. Thus began the idea of advocacy and ultimately a separate profession of lawyers.

While there may be good and bad lawyers, just like there are good and bad plumbers, a lawyer can assist not only in advocating your interests but also in protecting your rights. A classic example is your last will, in which you determine how to distribute your worldly goods after death. A lawyer can assist you in drafting the appropriate document.

Criticisms of lawyers often centre on the use of archaic terms. The use of legal terms is slowly giving way to plain language, as evidenced by insurance contracts that have become more and more readable. This is a direct result of the public's demand for straightforward language.

The more the public demands this simple language, the more the legal profession will adopt it, if only for self-preservation.

In Canada, the system of justice is administered by federally and provincially appointed judges in every province and territory. It is no longer the case that the king or queen alone can dispense justice, given the size and complexity of our society. There are over 1,000 federally appointed judges who have the mandate of interpreting the laws passed by Parliament. They also settle individual disputes as they come before the courts.

Most provinces and territories have an entry-level court, often called a superior court. The superior court handles most disputes. If the parties are not satisfied with the result, there are provincial appeal courts that review and, if necessary, reverse the lower court's decision. The ultimate appeal court is the Supreme Court of Canada, which hears appeals from the provinces in both civil and criminal matters.

Judges are often criticized for making erroneous decisions or creating new laws, a domain traditionally reserved for Parliament. It is often suggested that those decisions are direct results of the input made by clients and their lawyers. If a client fails to tell a lawyer the full story, then the results can often be skewed. Similarly, if a lawyer fails to fully advance all relevant legal arguments, then a court cannot be blamed for rendering a decision that may not cover all issues. As a result, it is vital that individuals fully disclose their problems to their solicitors. To encourage full disclosure, the concept of solicitor-client privilege, similar to the privilege between a priest and a penitent, has been developed. The information given to a lawyer remains confidential and fully protected by law. In this fashion, a lawyer can be armed with all the relevant facts and protect or advance a client's interests to the fullest.

The fear often expressed by clients is that, if they tell the full story, a lawyer may refuse to take the case. A lawyer, and ultimately a court, must be armed with all the facts to properly solve a legal problem. Full disclosure is essential to this process and must be encouraged.

Criticism has been levied against lawyers for taking too much time explaining the law in a particular case. What I hope to do with this book is offer basic information on various areas of the law and provide answers to the most frequently asked questions. I hope that the book will assist readers in demystifying the law and understanding its basic concepts.

The questions that follow have been frequently asked by clients and CBC Radio listeners. Each section explains a legal concept, followed by the basic questions and answers in each area. You will also see inserts that provide further explanations, legal trivia, or stories to illustrate points. I also hope to debunk a few legal myths.

There are three books in the series. What I hope to do in book one is explain the legal system and individual rights. In book two, I will cover issues surrounding the family and buying a home. Finally, in book three, I will cover retirement and estate planning. In this way, I will cover an individual's life, at least from a legal point of view, from birth to death.

Remember, every case is different, and every new fact puts a wrinkle in the case. Provincial laws vary and often change. This book should be used as a guide and not necessarily the definitive solution to each situation. Yet basic principles can be explained and are applicable in many day-to-day situations.

CHAPTER ONE

Property Rights

Long before our current system of land registration, there was a ceremony involved in the purchase of a piece of land. You would go to the property, and the vendor would take a clump of earth and gently toss it at you. This was effectively the way of transferring property from one person to another. Since disputes often arose as to whether this act of throwing sod had actually taken place, the king or queen would have a parchment prepared by one of his or her loyal scribes. This parchment was your proof of ownership. Eventually, a system of registration developed because copies of these parchments would be either lost or destroyed.

Land ownership has formed an essential part of society for thousands of years, partly because it confers wealth. Unfortunately, disputes over issues such as rights-of-way, rights to water, and boundaries continue to this day. However, instead of disputing a cow's right-of-way over a field, people now dispute a car's right-of-way between houses.

Land ownership continues to be important, and buying your first home is probably one of your largest investments. Often the emotional heart overtakes the logical mind when it comes to home ownership. Yet once the dust settles and the last box is unpacked, your focus changes, and issues surrounding fences and neighbours take over. Here are some of the issues on people's minds.

Neighbours and Property Lines

Q: One neighbour's well is 100 feet deeper than the other neighbour's well. As a result, water is draining into the deeper well. What recourses are available?

A: When you own a piece of property, you are required to use it in a peaceful manner, without disturbing your neighbour. Disturbances usually involve noise, and you cannot disturb your neighbour's peaceful enjoyment of his or her property by playing loud music. In a similar fashion, if some item on your property causes damage to your neighbour, then you are required to fix the problem. In this case, since the well of one neighbour affects that of the other, corrections are required so that each landowner does not affect the other's rights to water.

Q: What are property owner's rights on overhanging trees?

A: Property lines can be pictured as not only the lines surrounding the property but also the virtual lines from the ground up, past the roof line. Therefore, if trees overhang onto a neighbour's property, the neighbour is entitled to cut the overhanging branches. The one condition is that you cannot damage the tree by cutting those branches.

The expression **since time immemorial** actually has a legal basis. Time immemorial is defined as the time prior to the commencement of the reign of Richard I of England in A.D. 1189. So, when you say "since time immemorial," it really means something.

Q: How close to a property line can a shed be built?

A: Most municipalities have regulations that govern how close to a neighbour's property small structures can be built. In Ottawa, buildings that are less than 100 square feet must be two feet away from the property line. Anything above 100 square feet requires a building permit and setbacks depending on local zoning.

Q: A fence was built inside a neighbour's property line, but the neighbour attempted to obtain the other neighbour's contribution toward the cost of building the fence. What is each owner's respective right?

A: If the fence is built on a property line, each neighbour must agree on the design and the height and share equally in the cost. If the fence is built within a property line, however, then it is totally the responsibility of the neighbour building the fence.

Q: A neighbour was shooting squirrels from his porch, and bullets were crossing into a neighbour's property, where children were playing. Can this activity be stopped?

A: Subject to municipal or rural rules on the use of firearms, a person is entitled to protect his or her property. However, if doing so interferes with another neighbour, then the activity is improper. This is especially so when the activity endangers the lives of the neighbour's children.

In Quebec, the law used to provide a right to chase animals. Article 428 of the pre-1994 Civil Code read as follows:

Pigeons, rabbits and fish which go into another dove-cote, warren or pond, become the property of him to whom such pond, warren or dove-cote belongs, provided they have not been attracted there by fraud or artifice.

Bees living in a state of freedom are the property of the person discovering them, whether or not he be the proprietor of the land on which they have established themselves.

Whenever a swarm of bees leaves a hive, the proprietor may reclaim them, so long as he can prove his right of property therein, and he is entitled to take possession of them at any place on which they may settle, even if such place be on the land of another person, provided, however, that he notify the proprietor of such land and compensate him for such damages, and unless the swarm settles in a hive which is already occupied, in which case the proprietor loses all right of property in such swarm.

Q: Two individuals are sharing a house and expenses. How do they protect their own interests?

A: The parties should set down on paper their respective rights and obligations concerning the house and its expenses. Doing so should prevent disputes about each person's rights and obligations.

Q: A neighbour suspects another neighbour of videotaping the activities of all adjoining homeowners. What can be done?

A: Taking pictures of another person in his or her backyard is an invasion of privacy. The homeowner may well deny that he or she is taking pictures; however, if all the neighbours have seen the video-taping going on, then they should write a polite letter to the homeowner asking him or her to stop. If the activity continues, the police should be contacted. Alternatively, they can sue, asking for destruction of the camera and videotapes since their privacy has been invaded.

Squatter's Rights

Squatter's rights is the common term for someone occupying another person's piece of property. You can acquire squatter's rights for land owned by a government, but it takes 60 years. For example, if your family has used a piece of government land, and has had it fenced, continuously and openly for 60 years, then you can claim ownership.

This happened in a recent case with a piece of land that was not used by the government. When the homeowner attempted to fence the property after many years of use, the neighbours objected and burned his house down. The lesson: you may be able to exert squatter's rights against the government, but you must not offend your neighbours.

Q: A neighbour wishes to erect scaffolding outside his property lines. There has been a history of problems with this homeowner. Can the adjacent landowner object to the scaffolding or insist that it be erected only if a new privacy fence is built between the two properties?

A: The adjacent landowner can prevent access to his property but cannot force a neighbour to build a fence. If a fence is built on the property line, it must be agreed to in terms of both style and cost. Generally, there is a 50/50 sharing of costs if the fence is on the property line. If it is to be built within the property line, then the homeowner can choose the style and set the price since he is solely responsible for it.

So that everything is clearly understood if scaffolding is to be erected, the neighbours should write up a small agreement setting out who is to do what and that the scaffolding and repairs are to be undertaken at the expense of only one neighbour. Make sure that the agreement contains the provision that the neighbour cleans up after the work has been completed.

Q: What are my rights when a neighbour keeps old cars and tires on his lawn, causing unsightly views and hindering me from enjoying my property?

A: You should contact the local building inspector, who can inform you about local by-laws and rules. In an urban area, there are laws governing abandoned cars and tires left on a property. If the local officials do nothing, the province may step in, especially since tires are considered a fire hazard. In that case, you should contact the Ministry of the Environment.

Q: A local school board built an addition to a school well within the property lines. However, the renovations block some of the sunlight. What can be done?

A: The first step is to write a letter to the school board setting out your concerns. Generally, the board will attempt to reach a resolution by giving you monetary compensation. The addition interferes with your property rights, which include the right to light. If the problem goes unanswered, you can consider suing for the loss of value in the property as well as the loss of light. Oil companies often compensate adjoining landowners when renovations to existing gas stations are made. It is no different here with the school board.

Q: Before purchasing a property, the prospective homeowners hired a house inspector. Other than some minor problems, the inspector certified the home as being fit. Problems arose relating to condensation around windows and the drainage system. What can be done?

A: If it turns out that the windows or sewage system was defective prior to the purchase, then the house inspector is liable. If the problem is more recent, then the inspector isn't liable. The question is whether the homeowners go ahead and make the repairs and sue afterward or contact the inspector to have the problem fixed at his or her expense. They should also consider suing (if they don't agree to compensate you) the previous owner, who may have failed to disclose these problems in the contract of sale.

Mortgages

Q: A property was sold by the first mortgage holder, and there was a shortfall that did not cover a second mortgage. What is the owner's obligation to pay the second mortgage?

A: A mortgage is nothing more than confirmation of a debt registered against a piece of property. If there has been a default in payment, either mortgage holder can sell the property to recover money. If the first mortgage holder sells the property and there is insufficient money to pay the second mortgage, the owner is still responsible for it since it confirms a preexisting obligation.

Q: How do I arrange for a 90% mortgage?

A: Most financial institutions will lend up to 75% of the value of a property with a mortgage. If a higher level of financing is required, then one option is to obtain a second mortgage. Another is to obtain government insurance up to 90% of the value through an agency called the Canadian Mortgage and Housing Corporation. Most financial institutions will arrange for an application to CMHC. After this insurance is obtained, the financial institution will lend you 90% of the value.

FROM THE ONTARIO SUPERIOR COURT
IN THE CASE OF YAMADA vs. MOCK
JUNE 7, 1996

FROM THE JUDGMENT OF DAY J.:

Facts

Defendant third party claimant, Martin Mock, as mortgagee, retained third party Gerald Miller, a solicitor, to act on his behalf with respect to a third mortgage at 132 Geoffrey Street, Toronto (the "Geoffrey Street property"). Mr. Miller acted on both sides of the transaction. He took instructions from third party Say Van Nguyen and was advised by Mr. Nguyen that the mortgage was on the matrimonial home of Mr. Nguyen and his wife Saeko Yamada, title to the home being in the name of Mrs. Yamada. The mortgage was a forgery in that the signature of the mortgagor, Mrs. Yamada, was signed by a woman posing to be her as the spouse of Nguyen.

Mr. Miller had acted for Mr. Nguyen and the impostor on previous occasions all the while not being aware that the impostor was anyone other than Mr. Nguyen's wife. He never made inquiry of Mr. Nguyen or the person purporting to be Mrs. Yamada on prior occasions.

Analysis

I focus on the foreseeability of the risk. What should a solicitor be expected to foresee? Should a solicitor anticipate that the person before him in a transaction with major financial consequences may be an impostor? While the solicitor should not be expected to act as guarantor, he or she should take reasonable steps to protect the interest of the party which he or she is serving. While the eliciting of identification may not prevent fraud, it would make it much more difficult. The likelihood of someone producing false documentation is far less than someone simply asserting that they are someone other than who they are. It would have been an easy step to take. Both parties are innocent. As between them, who should bear the risk? Mr. Miller could have easily sought identity; there is nothing Mr. Mock could have done.

Finding

I find that the failure to ask for identification is below the standard of care of solicitors in this situation. Indeed, if the practice were not to ask for identification in such circumstances, I see the risk in these circumstances to be plainly foreseeable and, regardless of the practice, the law would impose liability on the solicitor to deal with the foreseeable risk.

Q: I am paying off my mortgage, what actions must I take with my bank or trust company?

A: When the last payment has cleared, apart from celebrating the fact that you are mortgage-free, you should get a **discharge of mortgage** from the bank. This preprinted government form must be registered against your property. Originally, when the mortgage was granted, it was registered against your property, and this new document discharges and cancels that mortgage. It clears up the title so that you can sell your property free and clear of any debt. The cost of registering the document is $50 in Ontario, and it is registered at the local registry office.

SAMPLE MORTGAGE FORM

Charge/Mortgage of Land
Form 2 - Land Registration Reform Act

Province of Ontario

B

(1) Registry ☐ Land Titles ☐	(2) Page 1 of ___ pages

(3) Property Identifier(s)	Block	Property	Additional: See Schedule ☐

(4) Principal Amount

Dollars $

(5) Description

New Property Identifiers — Additional: See Schedule ☐

Executions — Additional: See Schedule ☐

(6) This Document Contains	(a) Redescription New Easement Plan/Sketch ☐	(b) Schedule for: Description ☐ Additional Parties ☐ Other ☐	(7) Interest/Estate Charged Fee Simple

(8) Standard Charge Terms - The parties agree to be bound by the provisions in Standard Charge Terms filed as number ___ and the Chargor(s) hereby acknowledge(s) receipt of a copy of these terms.

(9) Payment Provisions

(a) Principal Amount $	(b) Interest Rate ___ % per annum	(c) Calculation Period

(d) Interest Adjustment Date	Y	M	D	(e) Payment Date and Period		(f) First Payment Date	Y	M	D

(g) Last Payment Date				(h) Amount of Each Payment	Dollars $

(i) Balance Due Date				(j) Insurance	Dollars $

(10) Additional Provisions

Continued on Schedule ☐

(11) Chargor(s) The chargor hereby charges the land to the chargee and certifies that the chargor is at least eighteen years old and that

....

The chargor(s) acknowledge(s) receipt of a true copy of this charge.

Name(s)	Signature(s)	Date of Signature Y	M	D

(12) Spouse(s) of Chargor(s) I hereby consent to this transaction.

Name(s)	Signature(s)	Date of Signature Y	M	D

(13) Chargor(s) Address for Service

(14) Chargee(s)

(15) Chargee(s) Address for Service

(16) Assessment Roll Number of Property	Cty.	Mun.	Map	Sub.	Par.	Fees

(17) Municipal Address of Property	(18) Document Prepared by:	Registration Fee

Total

05-359 (1295) DPP

SAMPLE MORTGAGE FORM

DYE & DURHAM CO. INC.—Form No. 980
Amended NOV. 1992

Province of Ontario

Discharge of Charge/Mortgage
Form 3 — Land Registration Reform Act

C

(1) Registry ☐ Land Titles ☐ (2) Page 1 of ___ pages

(3) Property Identifier(s) Block Property Additional: See Schedule ☐

(4) Description

FOR OFFICE USE ONLY

New Property Identifiers Additional: See Schedule ☐

(5) Charge to be Discharged

Registration Number Date of Registration Y M D

(6) This is a

Complete Discharge ☐ Partial Discharge ☐ Final Partial Discharge ☐

(7) Description (cont'd.), Recitals, Assignments

Continued on Schedule ☐

(8) Chargee(s) I am the person entitled by law to grant the discharge and this charge is hereby discharged as to the land described herein.

Name(s) Signature(s) Date of Signature Y M D

Additional: See Schedule ☐

(9) Chargee(s) Address for Service

(10) Document Prepared by:

FOR OFFICE USE ONLY

Fees

Registration Fee

Total

Percentage Clauses

Many people are familiar with a straight residential mortgage. A bank or trust company loans you money, and you repay the loan on a monthly basis. In commercial situations, banks and trust companies often lend money to a business at a preferential rate and require the business to pay them a percentage of profits or rentals on a certain building. (This type of clause, called a **percentage clause**, often appears in commercial leases in which landlords require a base rent and a percentage of sales.) It is rare, but it does occur in commercial mortgage situations. Since it is rarely used, banks often forget that such a clause exists and, in a recent case, attempted to recover years of percentage profits. They were partially successful in that they wanted the premiums for having lent the money at reduced rates, yet they did not want to put the company out of business. They compromised the amount that would otherwise have been payable to them. So much for the banks reading their own fine print.

RIGHT-OF-WAY

Q: What is a right-of-way, and what are the respective owners' rights?

A: A right-of-way is the right to use a driveway or laneway or road that passes between two properties. Each neighbouring owner is entitled to use that road without interfering with the other's right to use it. If one neighbour blocks access to it, then he or she is breaching the agreement on a right-of-way, and this agreement can be enforced in a court of law.

Q: How do I recover a lost right-of-way?

A: If a right-of-way has not been used for 60 years, then the right is lost. If the right-of-way is essential for access, then you can provide a court with evidence showing that this is the only way to access your property, and the court can determine whether the right-of-way should be granted. Once it is granted by court order, the order will be registered against the property to reaffirm the right-of-way.

Q: Who has the right to use a beach front?

A: Most deeds specify the right to use a beach front. If a deed does not specify this right, then an application will have to be made to the provincial or federal government authority (depending on who owned the beach originally) for the right to use that beach front.

Q: A beach-front recreational property borders on a provincial park. Users of the park use the private beach. What can be done?

A: If the owner of the property clearly has the right to the beach front, and there are no rights-of-way over that beach front, then the owner can post signs and if necessary erect a fence to prevent access to the property. The same applies if the cottage property is being leased, in which case the landlord will have to ensure that the tenant has access to the beach.

Property Surveys

Q: A property was sold without a survey being done first. A new survey was done, and the new owner ended up with less property. Can she sue the previous owner?

A: If the sale took place on a "as is, where is" basis (i.e., there were no promises), then the new owner has to suffer the loss. However, if the square footage or acreage was an essential part of the purchase, then she can either have the purchase cancelled or have the price reduced.

Q: After a property sale, it was discovered that a well was actually located on a neighbour's property. What are the parties' rights?

A: If the well formed an essential part of the agreement, then the purchase price can be reduced or the sale cancelled. Alternatively, the neighbour can be approached to determine whether he or she will allow the well to be used by the homeowner.

Q: A survey revealed that a fence was not properly placed on the property line. What can be done?

A: If the fence is outside a property boundary, then the neighbour can insist that it be moved to the property line. Expenses incurred may be recoverable from the previous owners if they made assurances about the location of the fence.

If you bought land in England, you would get "feoffment" (i.e., the right to feudal land) with "livery" (i.e., delivery of the land) of "seisin" (i.e., it would be yours forever).

Deeds

Q: Do I have to reregister a deed to land given changes in the registry system in Ontario?

A: All land in Ontario is registered. There are two systems of registration. One is a computerized system, and one is a manual system. Ontario is slowly converting to a computerized system. The government will take care of computerizing the registration system, and no individual will be required to reregister deeds. If you have a concern about the title of your property once the system is computerized, you can visit the registry office in your city or town and obtain a printout showing that you are the owner of your property.

Selling Property

Q: An individual lives in Ontario but has cottage property in Quebec. Can an Ontario lawyer deal with the property in the event of its sale?

A: In Ontario, all lawyers can handle real estate transactions. In Quebec, however, there is a "split profession." Some lawyers go to court, and others, called **notaries**, handle real estate matters. As a result, if you wish to sell a cottage property in Quebec, you must hire a notary, who is a lawyer by training but has restricted his or her practice to the preparation and registration of deeds. An Ontario lawyer, even if he or she is a member of the Quebec bar, cannot deal with the sale of your property unless also registered as a notary.

Q: What is land transfer tax, and are any rebates available?

A: **Land transfer tax** is a system of taxation based on the value of your property when it is sold. These taxes must be remitted to Ontario, and in specific situations rebates may be available. For a while, the government had an incentive program to stimulate the purchase of real estate and granted rebates to first-time home buyers. The rebate program no longer exists.

Latent Defects

Q: Renovations were done to a house. Some time after, problems developed with the construction. Can the builder be sued?

A: In general, your right to sue is limited to six years. If problems have developed that could not have been discovered earlier, they may be considered **latent defects:** problems that only come to light later. If this is the case, then the builder can be sued for inadequate renovations.

Q: An individual purchased a house seven months ago and has now been advised by the municipality that parts of the building contravene the building code. What remedies are available?

A: Most renovations require a building permit. As part of the building permit, the renovations or additions will be inspected by a municipal official. If all construction meets municipal specifications, then a certificate is issued, and the building will meet the current standards. If the inspection reveals problems, then they must be remedied in order to have the building comply with the building code. The obligation of a municipality when it approves a renovation has recently been the subject of a ruling. The Supreme Court of Canada has said that a municipality may be liable if it negligently approves a renovation.

Q: An individual purchased a home with an addition that is now sinking. Is the previous owner or the municipality that approved the construction liable?

A: If the building was approved but not built to municipal specifications, and if the owner acted improperly in having the renovations done, then both parties can be sued for the costs involved in fixing the addition.

Q: Before starting a new housing development, the developers appeared at a public meeting and explained their project and presented site plans. After a few changes to reflect concerns of the neighbours, the development progressed. After completion, some of the new homes were closer to the property lines than had originally been indicated on the plans. Local councillors are surprised that the homes did not conform to the site plans. What can be done?

A: Here are some general comments:

1. The buildings must comply with local by-laws, including those about the separation between properties and property lines.

2. If the developers made certain public promises, then they can be held liable for breaching those promises. They can be forced to pay compensation to all affected homeowners.

3. The site plans and subdivision plans are generally registered at the local registry office, and if the local town or municipality fails to enforce them it too can be held liable.

4. Since buildings are generally not torn down, adjacent homeowners can hope for monetary compensation since their property values have been affected.

Q: A house was built by workers who used spare parts from various job sites. The purchasers moved in and had no problems. The city inspected the property and certified it to be in accordance with the building code. Some years later, problems arose with the heating system. The original contractors refused to accept any responsibility. The lawyer who'd acted on the purchase indicated that it would cost more to sue than to undertake the repairs. The owners subsequently found out that the lawyer had worked with the builder who'd provided the "spare parts." What can be done?

A: First, the building inspector obviously failed to do his or her job. Second, the contractors obviously misled the purchasers as to the condition of the property. Third, the lawyer who acted for them on the transaction obviously did not disclose that he also worked with the supplier. I would suggest that the homeowners write a letter to all three parties asking for compensation. If they refuse to resolve the matter out of court, then the only alternative is to proceed with a lawsuit, preferably in small claims court.

Q: Potential customers often ask contractors if it would be cheaper to build without a permit. Contractors often advise their clients that it is better to have the building inspected so that everyone is satisfied. In the case of decks and fences, many municipalities require an inspection, even for a simple fence. In the event of renovation or construction being undertaken without a permit, can the municipality force a rebuilding of whatever the contractor has done?

A: If a town or municipality requires a permit based on local by-laws, and the homeowner refuses to get one, a contractor should get it in writing. That way, the homeowner cannot later complain and sue the contractor. This document is called a **waiver** and should clearly state that the owner does not want a permit and assumes all responsibility should there be problems. The homeowner should clearly agree to compensate the contractor for all costs or losses associated with a subsequent lawsuit brought by the town or municipality.

This agreement often "scares" the homeowner into getting a building permit. Remember, the town or municipality retains the right to have a structure torn down and redone in accordance with the building code. If the agreement is signed, then the town or municipality may go after the homeowner first and not the contractor.

Steps of a Legal Dispute

1. **Write it down:** Take the time to write out clearly what happened. The process of putting pen to paper will help you to collect your thoughts and give your lawyer the full picture.

2. **Speak to a friend:** Sometimes talking it out with a friend will help you with your choices. Maybe you haven't seen all sides of the problem. Maybe there is an obvious solution to your dilemma.

3. **Write a letter:** If you send a polite letter outlining your concerns, maybe you'll get a proper explanation or even an offer to resolve the dispute.

4. **See a lawyer:** Set up a brief meeting with your lawyer armed with your written story. It will save time, money, and aggravation. The lawyer will tell you if you have a case.

5. **Get a lawyer's letter:** If there is a case, have your lawyer write a letter. It may solve the problem at minimal expense.

6. **Sue:** If all else fails, you may have to sue.

7. **Mediate:** You can now mediate most disputes. Mediation gives you the chance to tell your story in an informal fashion, and it costs less than a lawsuit. You still hire a lawyer, but you can save both time and money by this process.

Q: An individual wishes to purchase a condominium that is yet to be built. She is unsure about what inquiries should be made, especially in light of news reports of leaky condos in British Columbia. What should she do?

A: Prior to anything being built, it is very much a "buyer beware" situation. There is nothing to inspect other than building plans, which can change. I would suggest that the track record of the developer be investigated, and, if it has the backing of a major financial institution, it should be contacted. If there are other buildings built by that developer, they should be checked. Finally, the builder can be checked through the Better Business Bureau, an organization that monitors businesses in Canada. Since it is always preferable to see what you are buying before you buy it, the best advice may be to wait and see.

Q: If a building is incorrectly constructed, what is the liability of the architect?

A: In Ontario, the Limitations Act limits negligence or breach of contract suits against architects to six years after the cause of action arises. Case law adds that a plaintiff who intends to sue cannot turn a blind eye to problems and sue some 20 years later. In other words, architects cannot be left hanging forever, wondering whether or not they will ever be sued for something they did years ago.

Q: In 1979, a room was added to a house. The renovations proceeded smoothly, and the owners were happy with them. Some years later, the owners commissioned a survey of their property, and it turned out that part of the addition had been built over an existing hydro easement. A hydro easement is the right of a utility to run wires over your property without having to pay you compensation. The owners intend to sell their property and are concerned that the new purchaser may object to the addition, necessitating further renovations. What should the owners do?

A: If the addition encroaches ever so slightly on the easement, they do not have to rip down the whole addition. The key is to tell any prospective purchasers that there is a slight encroachment so that, if they buy the property, they do so fully aware of any problems associated with it. Most hydro companies will not be concerned with a small encroachment since they can still run wires over the property. If, on the other hand, the encroachment crosses the property line, then the adjacent owner can demand that the renovations be redone to conform with the property lines.

Q: A couple purchased a home in Ontario. As a condition of the purchase, the builder was required to construct an elevated deck off the first floor of the house. The deck was not completed when the family moved into the home. Sliding doors were installed leading onto the deck. The doors were temporarily blocked since the deck was not completed. Eventually, another contractor was hired to finish the deck so that the building would meet all applicable building codes and so that the house could be sold later. The original builder subsequently declared bankruptcy. What can the owners do to recover their costs?

A: If the original plans for the building included a deck, then the city or town that inspected the property prior to the family moving in would be partially responsible for having approved it, even though it was improperly completed. Since the contractor is no longer in business, the only alternative is to attempt to recover some of the costs from the city or town. If the original plans did not include the deck, then the owners must bear the costs of finishing it.

Q: A couple had a house built but are not satisfied with it. There are many outstanding repairs required. They have attempted to have the builder fix the problems, but he is reluctant to undertake further repairs. What can be done?

A: A new home is generally covered by New Home Warranty plans. These plans, run by the provincial government, are meant to ensure that the home is built to building code specifications. The government agency will intervene and assist homeowners in ensuring that the repairs are done in accordance with the building code. Alternatively, homeowners can undertake repairs themselves and attempt to recover costs from the builders. Prior to any repairs being undertaken, proper estimates should be obtained from two or three contractors so that the original builder cannot complain later that the renovations were done at excessive costs. Give the builder one more chance; otherwise, undertake the repairs on your own or seek government action.

Privacy

Q: How can I stop solicitation at my home?

A: Anyone can ring your doorbell and try to sell you some product. One alternative is to post a sign on your door asking that no solicitations take place. You can also post a sign at the edges of your property indicating that it is private property and that trespassers are not allowed on it. However, the need for privacy must be balanced with the right of individuals to ring your doorbell if they have a lawful reason to do so. If you make exceptions for newspaper and mail delivery, then you may have to accept the possibility that others will come to your door.

Q: Can I do anything about noise coming from a neighbour's stereo?

A: Yes. Not only are there noise by-laws in most municipalities, but also you have the right to peaceful enjoyment of your property. If a neighbour is interfering with that enjoyment, you should first ask that the noise be reduced; if the problem persists, you may then have to consult a lawyer, who might commence legal proceedings on your behalf.

Landlord and Tenant

Q: Who gets the last month's rent if a lease is cancelled?

A: A lease often provides that the last month's rent is forfeited as damages to the landlord if the tenant cancels the lease before its term. However, if you are subletting your apartment with the landlord's consent, then the new tenant can either replace the rent deposit (the landlord would then issue a refund to you) or pay you the equivalent sum with the landlord's approval.

Q: A tenant was required to sign a new lease each year but not required to pay the face amount of the lease. Why was the landlord doing this?

A: Rent increases are often limited by provincial legislation. It applies even if a new tenant takes over a unit. A new tenant has the right to find out what the previous tenant was paying. The landlord was likely having leases prepared for larger amounts so that he or she could show a new tenant the lease and increase the rent based on the higher figure. This was improper.

Q: A room in a house was rented on a verbal agreement. Can the owner evict the tenant without a lease?

A: Although a lease should always be signed, even for a room, if no lease exists, then a tenant is considered to be on either a weekly or a monthly basis depending on how rent is paid. If it is a monthly basis, then on one month's notice the tenant can be evicted.

Q: A tenant was notified by the landlord that his lease would be terminated early because of excessive noise. When the matter first arose, the tenant contacted the property management company and told it that the noise was being caused by someone else in the building. What can he do?

A: The notice should indicate that the tenant can challenge it by responding in writing and asking for a hearing. He can argue that another tenant made the noise and that the management company has the wrong tenant and the wrong unit. If the notice is silent on his right to object, then he can go to the provincial rental board, which will help him challenge the notice. The clerks at the rental board will assist the tenant in completing the necessary forms and advising the landlord of the challenge. When it comes to a hearing, the tenant should be armed with as many witnesses as possible to bolster his case and show that he wasn't the cause of the problem.

Q: An individual rented the back room of an apartment to a friend. Since she was a friend, there was no written agreement. The new tenant asked when she should start paying rent. Since most leases in the area ran from May 1, she was told that she could start paying from the date in May when she actually moved in. Unfortunately, the parties now dispute whether this discussion took place. Things did not work out, and a few months after moving in she moved out. Because there were no other

prospective tenants, rent was requested for May 1 to April 30 of the next year, even though she moved out prior to that time. It is now one person's word against the other's as to when rent was due. What should be done?

A: Without a written lease, it is one person's word against the other's, and that the renter was a friend only complicates matters. A letter should be written clearly stating that the rent is due and should be paid. If an unsatisfactory reply is received and the parties cannot settle their differences, then the only alternative is to take the matter to small claims court. The best advice is to put things down on paper, even between friends.

Q: Is a superintendent liable for damages to a tenant's bicycle?

A: If the bicycle was safely locked and out of the way of traffic, then the building owners and/or the superintendent can be held liable if they damage the bicycle. I would suggest attempting to negotiate a settlement since there is a fine line between asserting your rights and leaving matters as they stand in order to maintain good relations with your superintendent.

Q: After moving into a rented house, a young child fell onto a stone floor inside the house and fractured her skull. The fall was caused by faulty construction, and it turned out that the house hadn't been built in accordance with the building code. What can the renters do?

A: A landlord is required to provide a safe environment, and obviously this was not done. In all likelihood, the landlord would be liable for the injury suffered by the child. The landlord should be contacted as soon as possible so that he or she is made aware of the danger and can take appropriate measures. If you sit on your rights, then the landlord may well deny responsibility since there is no way to prove that the injury occurred as a result of faulty construction. If there is a lease, then the tenants need not worry about being evicted for raising a safety concern.

Q: A mother died, leaving some land in Quebec to her children. One of the children, now married, lives in Ontario. If she were to die, who would inherit her share?

A: Here are some general rules. If a child is given property, she can dispose of it under her will. The gift from her mother may contain restrictions that require the land to remain in her family, and they would exclude anyone else from inheriting that piece of property. In the event of a divorce, the daughter can claim the land as an inheritance and exclude it from matrimonial property that would otherwise be divided between the spouses. The issue of the land should be discussed between the spouses, and they should determine who will inherit it on death. If necessary, a specific clause should be added to the daughter's will. It would show all concerned parties that the issue has been discussed and properly dealt with under the will.

Q: What exposure do tenants face when they cancel leases early?

A: A lease is a legal contract whereby a tenant is required to pay the landlord a certain sum of money for a certain period of time. If the tenant wishes to cancel the lease early, then he or she may be liable for the full amount of the lease, though it may provide for a one-month penalty on cancellation. If a subtenant is found, then liability for the balance of the lease can be reduced.

Q: Who is responsible for water damage, an owner or a tenant?

A: If the damage is caused by the tenant, then the tenant is responsible. If the damage is caused by the landlord or the plumbing systems that belong to the landlord, then he or she is responsible.

Q: Who is responsible for environmental problems on leased premises?

A: Generally, both the landlord and the tenant can be held responsible for environmental damage on a property. If the tenant is unavailable, then ultimately the landlord will have to pay.

Q: Is a landlord required to pay interest on a last month's rent deposit?

A: Yes. Most provinces provide for the rate of interest due on last month's rent held by the landlord.

Joint Ownership

Q: Partners own a lot, and one wishes to buy out the other. The other person refuses to sell. What resources are available?

A: One partner should formally offer to buy out the other. This offer should be backed up with an appraisal of the value so that all parties are clear about what amount is due. Alternatively, if the partners have an agreement, it may provide for a mechanism to sell one party's interest. If the partner does not wish to sell, then a court can intervene and force the sale.

Recently, a court in Ontario had a novel approach to selling a partnership interest. Each party was put in a room. A stopwatch was started, with each side being given a set amount of seconds to prepare a written bid. This continued until one person bought out the other or could no longer afford to continue the bidding process. Although this approach was novel in Canadian law, it had the desired effect.

Q: How do I sell a jointly owned property when one of four siblings is holding up the process?

A: If the parties cannot agree, then the normal course is to have a lawyer start a legal proceeding to assess the property and provide for a mechanism to sell or buy any one person's interest.

Liability

Q: An individual received a bill for the previous owner's hydro expense. Who is responsible?

A: When you sell a piece of property, you are required to sign a document called an **undertaking** that guarantees you will pay for whatever expenses you incurred prior to the sale. This undertaking can be enforced in a court of law as a binding obligation to pay.

Q: There is damage to a rented water tank. Who is responsible?

A: If the tenant or owner damages a rental tank, then he or she is responsible. The utility providing the tank (hydro) is not responsible for any damages unless they are a result of a defect in the tank itself. If the installation was defective, then the installer may be responsible.

Q: Who is responsible for damages to a boat winterized in a marina?

A: If the damage was caused by neglect of the storage facility, then it is responsible for repairs. If you are required to winterize your boat by adding certain fluids and protecting it, then you are responsible for repairs.

Q: Who is liable for injuries at a sports event?

A: When you purchase a ticket to a sports event, there will likely be a clause on the back of the ticket that limits the responsibility of the sports facility. However, one cannot limit liability for negligence, nor can one limit liability if the injured person did not know that there was limited liability. If you are hit by a baseball while in the stands, then chances are, given the limited liability, that you cannot recover damages. If, however, a baseball player intentionally threw a bat or ball at you, then he or she would be liable both civilly and criminally (assault).

Q: Who is liable for damages to a car in a parking lot?

A: If the owners of the parking lot did not post signs limiting liability, and allowed vandals to enter an unsupervised lot, then the owners will be responsible for damages to your car. If, however, they have taken all reasonable safety precautions, including the posting of warning signs, then they are not responsible for damages to your car.

A certain Batman costume has the following warning: "For play only: mask and chest plate are not protective; cape does not enable user to fly." This type of label is meant to warn buyers that the costume is just a toy. It would limit the manufacturer's liability if someone actually tried to use the cape to fly.

Q: Who is responsible for injuries that occur in a neighbour's pool, and how does the neighbour reduce legal exposure?

A: Most municipalities require that pools be fenced and appropriate locks be installed. If, however, someone scales the fence and uses the pool, then it could be argued that the trespasser is responsible. The best way to reduce legal exposure is to ensure that your fences meet height limits, that your locks are secure, and that your neighbours are told of the existence of your pool and the risks inherent if their children use it without permission.

Q: What legal steps are available to prevent a neighbour's dog from biting my children?

A: Municipal regulations often require dogs to be leashed or fenced in a secure area. If a dog escapes from a fenced area and injures a neighbour's child, then the dog's owner will be held responsible.

In the 1970s, every dog was entitled to one bite before its owner could be sued. This no longer applies.

Q: What is the weight of a nonresponsibility clause signed for a canoeing course?

A: Because of the nature of the activity, be it canoeing or white-water rafting (or for extreme sports), most organizers or teachers require that a nonresponsibility clause be signed. It provides that, in the event of an injury or accident, they will not be held responsible. Also, since you are involved in a high-risk activity, it is unlikely that a court will decide in your favour. The exception would be if the organizers or teachers were clearly negligent in planning or carrying out the activity.

Q: Who is responsible if horses damage property?

A: The owner of a horse is responsible for any damage caused should it, or for that matter any other animal, escape from a barn or closed field.

Q: Who is liable for damages to a rented cottage?

A: The tenants are responsible for all damages caused by their occupancy of the rented premises. If the damages were caused by some third person, however, that party may be held jointly responsible with the tenants.

Q: Who is liable for lost courier packages?

A: Couriers are responsible for lost packages. However, there may be clauses in the shipping documents that limit liability to either the cost of the parcel or the declared value, if such a value has been declared. The item's value should always be declared so that adequate compensation is paid.

Q: What is the liability of a real estate agent on the sale of a home?

A: Real estate agents may act for both the buyer and the seller. In that situation, they must be extremely careful in what they say. If they promise that the property has certain features, which it does not, then they can be held personally liable to the buyer. If each party has a real estate agent, then they must rely on their own agent. When people sell real estate, a certain amount of exaggeration may take place. In that scenario, it is "buyer beware," and you cannot fully rely on the statements made.

Q: Who is responsible for the theft of jewellery left on consignment?

A: Although you remain the owner of the item, the seller has agreed to keep a percentage of whatever is received. If the seller loses the item, then he or she is responsible for its full value.

Q: What is the right of a newspaper publisher to toss free newspapers onto a homeowner's driveway versus the homeowner's right not to have any home delivery or anyone trespass on the property? In one case, a homeowner went to the publisher's office to reinforce the request to stop delivery. The problem is that, with newspapers accumulating on the property, it appears that no one is at home, and the chance of vandalism increases.

A: The homeowner has the right to prevent people from trespassing on the property. By allowing home delivery of a newspaper, you give the publisher a "licence" to enter your property. If you do not wish to have newspaper delivery, and have clearly specified that wish to the publisher, then he or she is exposed to a lawsuit if delivery continues. The accumulation of newspapers is clearly a sign to vandals that you are not home. In the case mentioned above, the homeowner did the reasonable thing in going to the publisher to request that home delivery be stopped. If this activity continues, then the homeowner can go to court seeking an injunction prohibiting further deliveries. If the publisher breaches the injunction, then he or she may be faced with severe penalties and/or imprisonment.

Q: A local restaurant was converted to a dance hall and obtained a licence from town council to play music four nights a week. Inevitably, the noise became louder as the weeks and months went by. Complaints to the local bar owner were ignored, and the local police say that there is nothing they can do since the commercial establishment got a licence. What can the homeowner do?

A: Unfortunately, the time to object was when the business applied for the licence. It appears to be within its right to play music up to a certain time of night. However, if local residents present a signed petition to councillors (who are elected officials), they may place some new restrictions on the bar. Another approach would be to measure sound levels over time to see whether local noise by-laws are being breached.

Q: An individual recently won a decision from a local housing tribunal, but the landlord refuses to pay. A *garnishment* order (a legal document seizing money) was issued by the small claims court; however, when it was filed with the bank in an effort to seize the landlord's bank account, there was no money in the account. What can the individual do?

A: A garnishment order, as indicated, is a seizure of a specific sum of money and must be specific in naming the bank branch and account in question. It must also be timely. In other words, it must be received by the bank when there is still money in the account. If at the time it is received by the bank there is no money, then the garnishment has to be refiled with the bank on a regular basis until money is seized. Since the garnishment is a specific legal remedy, it must be exercised carefully.

Q: Who is responsible for accidents at work?

A: Generally speaking, when an accident takes place at work, the employer may have insurance to cover the injuries. If the accident was caused solely by the actions of the employee, then he or she is responsible.

Q: What are a bar owner's responsibilities when patrons drink and drive?

A: Bar owners must ensure that none of their patrons leaves in a drunken state and gets behind the wheel of a motor vehicle. It is often difficult, however, for injured persons to prove that they were only at one bar. If they went to a series of bars and drank at each one, then the last in the chain may be the only one responsible.

Q: On a street with a steep incline and a sharp curve, there is a "no parking" sign. Cars are typically parked on the curve despite the sign. On one snowy day, a driver was unable to avoid the parked cars and struck one of them. Is the city liable for not enforcing the sign or for inadequate road maintenance?

A: Based on a recent ruling of the Supreme Court, a city is liable if it undertakes to manage or regulate a particular activity. In this case, the city decided to regulate that stretch of roadway by posting a no-parking sign. It failed to enforce the no-parking zone and additionally created a hazard in failing to clear away the snow. Given these facts, the city may well be responsible for the car accident. The city will no doubt argue that it did its best to clear away the snow and ice and enforce its no-parking zone. I would recommend an action in small claims court. It is best to have updated pictures of the breach, and a warning letter should be sent to the city not only to patrol the area but also to claim damages without the need of going to court. Be aware, however, that some municipalities require you to give notice within seven or 10 days of a particular incident in order to sue.

Q: A homeowner wishes to sue a contractor for the improper installation of brick. The homeowner wishes to use small claims court but needs clarification of the steps to follow. What are the steps in suing in small claims court?

A:

1. Prepare a written statement setting out the nature of your claim and the amount that you are attempting to recover.
2. Go to the small claims court and obtain the proper form that says you are suing another person.
3. Have the claim verified at the court, and on payment of a fee it will give you a court file number and stamp your document. This stamp registers your document with the court.
4. Mail a copy of your claim to the person being sued. Keep a record of the place, date, and time that you mailed the claim.
5. The defendant will have a number of days to file a defence, and the court will notify you when the defence has been filed.
6. After the defence is filed, you can request a meeting with a small claims court judge. This is called a **pretrial**. It is a chance for you to discuss your case in an informal effort to resolve your differences with the other party.
7. If your problem remains unresolved, then a trial date will be set.

8. At the trial, bring all your documents and all your witnesses. The witnesses are key to proving your case if you have insufficient documents to support your position or if there are conflicting versions of events.
9. After hearing both sides of the story, the judge will consider everything that has been said and will render a judgment.
10. The judgment is good for 20 years; if unpaid, you can seize money owed to the person sued so that you can be compensated for the judgment.

Cottages

Cottages are places of memories. Families have been known to dissipate when the family cottage is sold. Many now wish to rekindle those memories, and as a result prices for cottages are rising. Owning a cottage has its joys, but there can be serious legal pitfalls. Here are some general questions and answers.

1. The usual agreements of purchase and sale of a cottage rarely allow a purchaser the chance to check with the local township about **future building plans**. This check is essential to ensure that no plans are being considered for a waste dump right next to your new cottage. Make sure before you sign that no major plans are in the works.

2. You need to know whether you have **road access**.
    a. Does a road exist?
    b. Is the road open year-round?

c. Who owns the land on which the road has been built?

d. Who pays for road maintenance and repair?

e. Is your right-of-way over the road registered or mentioned in your deed?

3. Can you **reinspect the property** before closing to ensure that there has been no damage caused by the elements since you first saw the property?

4. Is the **sewage system** working, and have all the necessary permits been obtained?

5. Who owns the **lake bed** fronting your cottage, and who owns the **beach front**? In Ontario, most beaches are owned by the Crown because there were no roads when the province was in its infancy. The Crown therefore reserved 66 feet in width to allow settlers to travel from one end of the province to another. Here are some general rules:

   a. For nonnavigable waters, the lake bed is owned by the person who owns the cottage.

   b. For navigable waters, the lake bed is owned by the Crown.

   c. For inland nontidal waters, you own up to the water's lowest mark.

   d. For tidal waters, you own up to the high-water mark.

   This is of course **subject to your particular deed** giving you certain rights.

6. It's best to hire a **lawyer who practises near your cottage** since he or she may know of pitfalls peculiar to the region.

7. After you move in, don't move the **surveyor's stakes** (it's an offence punishable by fines if you do), and **don't shoot** squirrels from your porch (the bullets may trespass onto your neighbour's property).

Oh, the joys of cottage life can easily be ruined by a lawyer.

Q: A senior couple recently sold a cottage property. Must they declare a capital gain on the sale, and if so can they split it between husband and wife?

A: From a legal point of view, the couple must declare a capital gain under the Income Tax Act unless the cottage is their only property and has been designated as their principal residence. It used to be that each person in a couple could claim a separate principal residence (and sell it tax free), but that tax loophole has now been closed. If the property was owned jointly by husband and wife, then each can claim part of the gain; however, if it was owned by only one spouse, then he or she has to claim the gain. The best advice is to consult an accountant for your tax situation.

Q: An individual is considering buying a house in Ontario. He has never bought, owned, or sold a house in Canada, but he owns a house in the United Kingdom. That house is currently rented. Does he qualify as a first-time Canadian home buyer?

A: If he intended to relocate to Ontario and has taken up residency in the province, then, when he purchases a home for the first time, he is considered a first-time home buyer under Ontario law. The law is meant to encourage purchases in Ontario by people who have never owned property in the province. If there are government subsidies available at the time of purchase, then the application form will have to be reviewed. If the form asks specifically whether or not he has owned a home anywhere in the world, then he must say "yes." If there are no specific questions about previous home ownership worldwide, then he is considered a first-time home buyer.

Q: An individual living in Ontario was advised by a local municipal clerk that, if one uses land belonging to another person in an open fashion and improves it, such as erecting a fence, then he or she may make a claim of ownership after one year. Is this correct?

A: You have to separate claims for improvements/repairs from ownership rights. A claim for improvements can be made against an adjacent owner within six years in Ontario from when the repairs were done. If that claim is not advanced, then it will be lost, and the adjacent owner will benefit from the repairs. As for a claim of ownership, if you use a piece of land openly for 40 years, then you can apply to have it declared your own. If the land is owned by the government, then it takes 60 years of open use before you can claim ownership.

Q: A property owner encountered problems with the local municipality. For a number of years, she never received a property tax notice, but eventually she received a notice that her property would be put up for sale by the municipality since no taxes had been paid. As soon as she received that notice, she paid the taxes, which included penalties and interest for past years. What can property owners do to prevent additional interest and penalties from accumulating on their tax bills?

A: Property owners should check with the post office to make sure that their mail is being properly directed, check with their municipality to ensure that it has their correct mailing address, and ensure that both federal and provincial tax authorities have their

correct mailing address. Tax authorities often share address information, and it is important to ensure that each agency has the correct
address. If, after all that, the individual is still not getting her mail, then
she should write one last letter to the mayor of her municipality. She
should clearly say that she is the owner but that she has not received
proper tax assessments. If tax bills continue to get waylaid, then she
can go to court against the municipality seeking a declaration that
she is the owner of a piece of property with a correct mailing
address. She can sue for a refund of penalties and interest and for the
inconvenience caused by the municipality. With a lawsuit, the
municipality may take note of her correct address. If the same thing
should happen in the future, she will have the court order to confirm
that she did everything within her power to ensure that she receives
prompt tax notices.

**Q: For over 20 years, cottagers used a logging road for access to their
property. The logging road was sold as part of an adjacent piece of
property, and the new owners have made improvements to the road.
They now insist that the neighbours not drag any trees or logs on the
road for fear that it will cause damage to it. Can the new owners place
restrictions on the road?**

A: Check whether a right-of-way over the road was registered
on the titles of adjacent property owners. If there is a right-of-way
registered, then adjacent owners are entitled to use the road. If
there is no right-of-way registered, then the owners of that road
can make whatever repairs they want to it.

If the only access to the cottage is on that road, then, even if it
is not registered on the titles of the adjacent properties, the cottage
owners have the right to use it. You cannot block access to someone's property even though you own that piece of land.

The best thing to do is to have all the adjacent owners agree to the rights and obligations connected with that road. If all agree, then set it down in writing and have that new document registered on title.

Q: A group of property owners bought land in a local village that allowed them to erect a dock. Some other villagers are petitioning council to have the dock removed. There are, therefore, competing interests, and council is leaning toward removal of the dock even though the owners are willing to pay the municipality a fee. What can be done?

A: Municipalities cannot act arbitrarily, favouring one group over another. If they do, they can be sued. It sounds like council is caught between two competing interests. It then becomes a question of drafting petitions and lobbying local politicians so that most residents are satisfied. Remember that a council is elected, and, if enough people sign the petition, the municipality will respond.

Q: A neighbour severed some acres in the back of his property. The province concerned imposed some restrictions, including plans for a road. To date, the road has not been opened. The local municipality also intends to undertake some rezoning. Certain homeowners are concerned that this rezoning will breach the provincial conditions. What can be done?

A: The provincial conditions placed on the road do not expire at the whim of a municipality. If the municipality undertakes changes that do not respect conditions imposed by the province, then an agency called the Municipal Board, which oversees municipalities, can become involved and ensure compliance. As a landowner, you are affected by these developments and have the right to enforce the laws as they affect your property.

Q: An individual agreed to purchase a cottage and gave the owners a down payment. In an effort to avoid paying real estate fees, the owners sold the property to a family member, who then sold it to the individual for the balance of the purchase price. Some years have passed, and the individual now wishes to sell the cottage and pay capital gains taxes on the full value, not just on the balance of the purchase price. What should she do?

A: Under the Income Tax Act, capital gains taxes are due on secondary residences. The tax is based on the increased value from the time of purchase. The Income Tax Act also frowns on transfers between family members as a method of avoiding taxes. Therefore, from the Revenue Agencies' point of view, taxes are due on the full purchase price, including the initial deposit. The necessary documents should be obtained from the seller's lawyer. The real estate broker has the right to sue since the transfer was nothing more than a scheme to avoid paying real estate fees.

Q: A tree on a cottage property overhangs a neighbour's property, and the tree is dying. The cottage owner wishes to take down the tree, thereby avoiding damage to the neighbour's cottage. Can he do so without the neighbour's consent, and can he go onto the neighbouring property to remove branches?

A: As long as the tree is within your property, you have the right to manage it, which includes taking it down. You also have the right to enter your neighbour's property to remove the fallen branches. However, you should tell your neighbour of your plans, if only to avoid later disputes.

Q: A municipality has certain restrictions on building close to the waterfront. Existing cottages have buildings right up to the shoreline. Can a new building thus be built close to the water's edge?

A: Existing buildings are probably "grandfathered": they are allowed to stand because they have existed for quite some time. Check the municipal rules to make sure that the restrictions are on new buildings by new owners. Also check whether there is a provision allowing existing cottagers to build new structures close to the waterfront because they owned cottages prior to the new by-law taking effect.

Q: If the rights to a waterfront have been granted by the Crown to a property owner, what can she do to enforce her right to privacy?

A: Subject to local municipal regulations about the sizes of signs, she can erect signs indicating that it is private property and that no trespassing is allowed. She can also erect a fence in order to assert her ownership. Force cannot be used (except in certain specific situations), and in the event of trespass or trouble the police should be called.

Q: How can I find out whether there is a right of access or a right to use a road?

A: Each province has a system of land registration whereby each lot is registered at the local registry office (usually found at the courthouse). If there is a right of access or a road allowance or any other right of property, then it should be registered at that office. Title searchers, professionals trained in searching land titles, should be hired to investigate the rights of property as they affect your land. If there is an unregistered agreement and it is found, then it should be registered.

By registering it, you are providing notice to all concerned that you have the right to travel over a certain piece of land.

Q: Can the owner of a road accessible to other cottagers allow it to fall into disrepair?

A: No. If adjacent owners have a right to use the road, then unless there is something contrary in the agreement covering access the owner must ensure that the road is maintained. The owner cannot let the road fall into disrepair. The owner can use the road, set certain conditions and restrictions as long as they are reasonable, and require adjacent owners to help pay for the maintenance. The owner cannot, however, let the road fall into such a state as to render the right of access useless.

Q: A cottager had a sewage and water system installed with access pipes going across a neighbour's property. An agreement had been drawn up allowing the construction to take place. The new owners of the adjacent property now wish to cancel the agreement. What are the parties' rights?

A: The right to have water and sewage cross a neighbour's property is called an **easement**, and, if there is an agreement, then it should be registered. If it is not registered, then a court application can be brought to have it accepted and ultimately registered. Subsequent owners will then be bound by this agreement.

Q: What is the right of portage, and can landowners block that right?

A: When most provinces were established, the only means of travelling was through their water systems. In the event of a blockage, there was a right to portage a canoe across land regardless of ownership. As the provinces developed, this right was either cancelled or restricted. Since the provincial government granted the right, it could cancel it as well. Therefore, we now have a patchwork system in Canada on the right of portage, and you should obtain maps from Parks Canada of the areas that you wish to travel. These maps should show whether the right of portage still exists.

Q: A government agency has offered a cottage owner the rights to purchase his beach front and lake bed, which are owned by the Crown. Does he have to purchase them?

A: As long as the government does not intend to sell the beach front and lake bed to a third party, there is no obligation to buy them. On the other hand, owning them would ensure not only access but also privacy. Be aware, however, that a sale price must be reasonable, and if necessary you should hire an independent appraiser to determine the real value.

Q: Am I required to pay for volunteer fire services in a cottage area?

A: Unless there is some municipal by-law requiring a levy to be paid by all cottage owners, there is no strict legal obligation to pay for such services. However, since many cottagers are at their cottages only on a part-time basis, the volunteer fire service is there to protect their property in their absence. A voluntary contribution would foster goodwill in the community.

CHAPTER TWO

Family and Divorce

Traditionally, courts dealt with property disputes, such as which landowner could rightfully claim a certain field for his cattle over another landowner. Jonathan Swift in *Gulliver's Travels* explained the court process by drawing on the example of a cow that was stolen by a neighbour. Swift explained that lawyers and the law had a strange way of solving problems. Instead of arguing that the cow was stolen, a lawyer would argue that, regardless of ownership, the neighbour should get the cow because he needed it more. According to Swift, this was classic legal reasoning.

Society has evolved greatly since the 17th century. Concepts such as children's rights, name changes, and divorce have come into play, and courts are frequently called upon to settle disputes associated with these concepts. Judges and lawyers are often required to sort out various problems centred on the family. Yet even Henry VIII, a century before Swift, asked a court, namely the English House of Lords, to affirm his many divorces. It is not surprising, therefore, that today the family remains at the core of our society and forms the subject of many a court docket.

The law has also advanced along with technology — the Internet has given rise to new legal issues. And because of increasingly complex financial matters, the concept of powers of attorney has evolved. These powers allow for one person to conduct another's affairs.

At the risk of sounding too traditional, once you have started on your career path, family planning usually comes next. Matters include marriage, name changes, children, and sometimes divorce. Here are some of the issues facing the family today.

Parental Responsibility

Q: Is there a legal responsibility to tell a man that he is about to become a father?

A: From a legal viewpoint, if there is a possibility that support will be sought, then it is best to tell the future father of the pregnancy. Otherwise, he may deny that he is the father and argue that he has no financial obligation. In addition, when a child is born, the mother is required to register the child. She is asked on the registration form to name the father. It is an offence to lie or conceal information.

Q: What is the responsibility of a parent with a 10-year-old who uses a "psychic line" on a home phone?

A: Parents or guardians are fully responsible for the actions of dependent children. In this case, the phone will have been registered in the parent's or guardian's name. The parent or guardian is therefore responsible for anyone using that phone and incurring charges on it. This issue extends to use of the Internet. If a child accesses a restricted site, the child not only leaves a footprint of his or her address but may also order a product or cause a credit card to be used. As a parent, you are responsible for the actions of your child.

Q: How do I prevent an ageing parent from disposing of property?

A: If an elderly parent is unable to handle his or her affairs, then the family can appoint a family member or a third person as the aged person's power of attorney. This individual will then have some control over the property in question. Financial institutions will be advised of this change in status and take steps to prevent unauthorized withdrawals.

Marriage and Names

In Quebec, you can keep your married name, your maiden name, or a hyphenated combination of them. A child can use a hyphenated combination of both the father's and the mother's names. When children marry, they can choose a further-hyphenated name or keep the hyphenated maiden name.

For example, if Smith marries Jones, the spouse can be called Smith or Jones or Smith-Jones or Jones-Smith. If the child of Smith-Jones marries an Alfred, the child can be Smith-Jones-Alfred, Jones-Smith-Alfred, Alfred-Jones, Alfred-Smith, et cetera.

With so many possible combinations, it would be difficult five or six generations hence to tell who is related to whom by just looking at a name.

Name Changes

Q: Do I always have to use my legal name?

A: If you are known by a certain name, then you can use it in most transactions. If you signed for some product, then you are responsible to pay for it regardless of the name used. On certain legal documents, such as deeds to land, your legal name is required.

Q: How do I correct a name on a birth certificate?

A: Governments keep records of all births and issue birth certificates. If you want to correct an error or make a change, you simply apply to the names branch of the government. With the reason for the change set out on the appropriate form, and on payment of a small fee, the change will be made.

Q: Can a couple change their children's names given remarriage?

A: Yes. In the same way as correcting an error, with the appropriate form and fee the change can be made. Name changes are a provincial responsibility. In Ontario, they are handled by the names branch located in Sault Sainte Marie (consult the blue pages of your phone book for the department's name and address in your province). The fee is currently set in Ontario at $25, and there is no limit to the number of times that you can change a name.

Q: How do I change my name, and am I responsible for debts incurred under my old name?

A: Again, names can be changed with a form and a fee. Yet even with a new name, you are still the same person who incurred the debts, so you are responsible for them. You will often see lawsuits with names separated by the letters *a.k.a.*, which mean "also known as."

There is an urban legend that the singer formerly known as Prince changed his name to avoid paying certain debts. This scheme wouldn't work in Canada, although theoretically you can change your name to a symbol or mark. The risk is that someone can use your mark and in effect forge your signature. It's not recommended.

Mistaken Identity

Q: A collection agency is hassling a person for a debt that he did not incur. The person has the same name as the real debtor. What can be done?

A: The first thing is to meet with the agency and provide a statement, with proof of identity, that he is not the person in question. If the hassling continues, he can involve the credit bureau or the provincial Ministry of Consumer and Corporate Relations. If all else fails, he may have to start a lawsuit and get a court to declare that he is not responsible for that particular debt.

Divorce

When spouses separate, there are in general three basic legal issues to be resolved. The first is to cancel the marriage, the second is to ensure that the spouses or any children are given monetary support, and the third is to distribute assets.

Many problems can be avoided with a domestic contract, which sets out the expectations of each party and covers many of the issues that arise in the event of a breakdown in the relationship. The contract sets out what each spouse has brought into the marriage, who will support the family and in what proportion, and what divisions of assets and responsibility occur in the event of a breakup. With the recent ruling by the Supreme Court of Canada on same-sex relationships, this contract now applies to all relationships.

With domestic contracts, the parties take the time to plan the future. If they don't, then divorce proceedings can get acrimonious since each side may have a different version of events. Take, for example, an inheritance. It may be agreed that the money will be used to buy a house and that on separation the party who received the inheritance will receive that amount out of any sale. Without a contract, the law will require a 50/50 split, so that the spouse receiving the inheritance forfeits 50% to the other spouse. It is therefore important to address these issues when relations are cordial.

Q: How do I get a divorce?

A: You should consult a lawyer, who will obtain the necessary information from you, including the particulars of your marriage and assets. Formal papers are then prepared and stamped by a court. They are sent to your spouse. If your spouse does not contest the divorce, then the papers are processed by court officials, and a divorce judgment is issued usually in a matter of weeks. If support and custody are issues, then there will be a dialogue with your spouse's lawyer, and you and your spouse may draft and sign a separation agreement, which will cover the divorce itself and the division of assets. If there is no agreement on any of the issues, then a court hearing will be requested, and the matter may take up to two years to resolve.

Q: How do I find out if my ex-spouse is making more money than disclosed?

A: When spouses get divorced, each must disclose assets and income. Often there will be supporting documents such as income tax returns. If there is other nonreported income, then your lawyer can apply to the courts to obtain further disclosure from your ex-spouse.

Q: After a four-and-a-half-year marriage, a couple wish to divorce, but they live in different provinces. Where should divorce proceedings be initiated?

A: The Divorce Act of Canada provides that divorce proceedings can be initiated in the jurisdiction of either party. The main issue is whether the proceedings are brought to the other spouse's attention by receipt of the divorce papers.

Q: A couple were married in Ontario and then lived most of their married life in the United States. One of the spouses has now retired to Ontario and wishes to apply for a divorce. Where should the divorce be granted?

A: Since one of the parties now lives in Ontario, courts there have jurisdiction over the application for a divorce, and the matter can be brought before Ontario courts.

Excerpts from the Divorce Act

JURISDICTION

3. (1) [**Jurisdiction in divorce proceedings**] A court in a province has jurisdiction to hear and determine a divorce proceeding if either spouse has been ordinarily resident in the province for at least one year immediately preceding the commencement of the proceeding.

DIVORCE

8. (1) [**Divorce**] A court of competent jurisdiction may, on application by either or both spouses, grant a divorce to the spouse or spouses on the ground that there has been a breakdown of their marriage.

(2) [**Breakdown of marriage**] Breakdown of a marriage is established only if

(a) the spouses have lived separate and apart for at least one year immediately preceding the determination of the divorce proceeding and were living separate and apart at the commencement of the proceeding; or

(b) the spouse against whom the divorce proceeding is brought has, since celebration of the marriage,

(i) committed adultery, or

(ii) treated the other spouse with physical or mental cruelty of such a kind as to render intolerable the continued cohabitation of the spouses.

SAMPLE DIVORCE PETITION

ONTARIO

Superior Court of Justice

⬡ **SEAL**

at _____
Court office address

Court File Number

Family Law Rules, O.Reg. 114/99

Form 8A: Application
(divorce) ☐ Joint
          ☐ Simple

Applicant(s)

Full legal name & address for service — street & number, municipality, postal code, telephone & fax numbers and e-mail address (if any).	Lawyer's name & address — street & number, municipality, postal code, telephone & fax numbers and e-mail address (if any).

Respondent(s)

Full legal name & address for service — street & number, municipality, postal code, telephone & fax numbers and e-mail address (if any).	Lawyer's name & address — street & number, municipality, postal code, telephone & fax numbers and e-mail address (if any).

☐ **THIS CASE IS A JOINT APPLICATION FOR DIVORCE. THE DETAILS ARE SET OUT ON THE ATTACHED PAGES.** The application and affidavits in support of the application will be presented to a judge when the materials have been checked for completeness.

☐ **IN THIS CASE, THE APPLICANT IS CLAIMING DIVORCE ONLY.**

TO THE RESPONDENT(S): A COURT CASE FOR DIVORCE HAS BEEN STARTED AGAINST YOU IN THIS COURT. THE DETAILS ARE SET OUT ON THE ATTACHED PAGES.

THIS CASE IS ON THE STANDARD TRACK OF THE CASE MANAGEMENT SYSTEM. No court date has been set for this case but, if you have been served with a notice of motion, it has a court date and you or your lawyer should come to court for the motion. A case management judge will not be assigned until one of the parties asks the clerk of the court to schedule a case conference or until a notice of motion under subrule 14(5) is served before a case conference has been held. If, after 200 days, the case has not been scheduled for trial, the clerk of the court will send out a warning that the case will be dismissed in 30 days unless the parties file proof that the case has been settled or one of the parties asks for a case conference or a settlement conference.

IF YOU WANT TO OPPOSE ANY CLAIM IN THIS CASE, you or your lawyer must prepare an answer (Form 10 — a blank copy should be attached), serve a copy on the applicant and file a copy in the court office with an affidavit of service (Form 6B).

YOU HAVE ONLY 30 DAYS AFTER THIS APPLICATION IS SERVED ON YOU (60 DAYS IF THIS APPLICATION IS SERVED ON YOU OUTSIDE CANADA OR THE UNITED STATES) TO SERVE AND FILE AN ANSWER. IF YOU DO NOT, THE CASE WILL GO AHEAD WITHOUT YOU AND THE COURT MAY MAKE AN ORDER AND ENFORCE IT AGAINST YOU.

If you want to make a claim of your own, you or your lawyer must fill out the claim portion in the answer, serve a copy on the applicant and file a copy in the court office with an affidavit of service.

You should get legal advice about this case right away. If you cannot afford a lawyer, you may be able to get help from your local Legal Aid office. *(See your telephone directory under LEGAL AID).*

_____   _____
Date of issue   *Clerk of the court*

Continued on next sheet

FLRS 8A (08/99)   (Français au verso)

SAMPLE DIVORCE PETITION

Court File Number

Form 8A: Application (divorce) (page 2)

FAMILY HISTORY

HUSBAND: Age: . . . .   Birth date *(d, m, y)*: . . . .

Resident in *(municipality & province)* . . . .

since *(date)* . . . .

Surname at birth: . . . .   Surname just before marriage: . . . .

Divorced before?   ☐ No   ☐ Yes. *(Place and date of previous divorce)* . . . .

WIFE: Age: . . . .   Birth date *(d, m, y)*: . . . .

Resident in *(municipality & province)* . . . .

since *(date)* . . . .

Surname at birth: . . . .   Surname just before marriage: . . . .

Divorced before?   ☐ No   ☐ Yes. *(Place and date of previous divorce)* . . . .

RELATIONSHIP DATES:

☐ Married on *(date)* . . . .   ☐ Started living together on *(date)*. . . . .

☐ Separated on *(date)* . . . .   ☐ Never lived together

THE CHILD(REN):

List all children involved in this case, even if no claim is made for these children.

Full Legal Name	Age	Birth date (d, m, y)	Resident in (municipality & province)	Now Living with (name of person and relationship to child)

PREVIOUS CASES OR AGREEMENTS

Have the parties or the children been in a court case before?

☐ No   ☐ Yes *(Attach a summary of court cases - Form 8E.)*

Have the parties made a written agreement dealing with any matter involved in this case?

☐ No   ☐ Yes *(Give date of agreement. Indicate which of its terms are in dispute. Attach an additional page if you need more space.)*

SAMPLE DIVORCE PETITION

Form 8A: Application (divorce) (page 3)

CLAIMS

USE THIS FRAME ONLY IF THIS CASE IS A JOINT APPLICATION FOR DIVORCE.

WE JOINTLY ASK THE COURT FOR THE FOLLOWING:

Claims under the *Divorce Act*

- 00 ☒ a divorce
- 01 ☐ spousal support
- 02 ☐ support for child(ren)
- 03 ☐ custody of child(ren)
- 04 ☐ access to child(ren)

Claims under the *Family Law Act or Children's Law Reform Act*

- 10 ☐ spousal support
- 11 ☐ support for child(ren)
- 12 ☐ custody of child(ren)
- 13 ☐ access to child(ren)
- 14 ☐ restraining/non-harassment order
- 15 ☐ indexing spousal support
- 16 ☐ declaration of parentage
- 17 ☐ guardianship over child's property

Claims relating to property

- 20 ☐ equalization of net family properties
- 21 ☐ exclusive possession of matrimonial home
- 22 ☐ exclusive possession of contents of matrimonial home
- 23 ☐ freezing assets
- 24 ☐ sale of family property

Other claims

- 30 ☐ costs
- 31 ☐ annulment of marriage
- 32 ☐ prejudgment interest
- 50 ☐ *(Other; specify.)*

USE THIS FRAME ONLY IF THE APPLICANT'S ONLY CLAIM IN THIS CASE IS FOR DIVORCE.

I ASK THE COURT FOR:

(Check if applicable.)

- 00 ☒ a divorce
- 30 ☐ costs

IMPORTANT FACTS SUPPORTING MY CLAIM FOR DIVORCE

☐ **Separation:** The spouses have lived separate and apart since *(date)*. . . . . and
    ☐ have not lived together again since that date in an unsuccessful attempt to reconcile.
    ☐ have lived together again during the following period(s) in an unsuccessful attempt to reconcile: *(Give dates.)*

☐ **Adultery:** *(Name of spouse)* . . . . has committed adultery.
(Give details. It is not necessary to name any other person involved but, if you do name the other person, then you must serve this application on the other person.)

☐ **Cruelty:** *(Name of spouse)* . . . . has treated *(name of spouse)*
. . . . with physical or mental cruelty of such a kind as to
make continued cohabitation intolerable. *(Give details.)*

SAMPLE DIVORCE PETITION

Court File Number

USE THIS FRAME ONLY IF THIS CASE IS A JOINT APPLICATION FOR DIVORCE.

The details of the other order(s) that we jointly ask the court to make are as follows: *(Include any amounts of support and the names of the children for whom support, custody or access is to be ordered.)*

IMPORTANT FACTS SUPPORTING MY OTHER CLAIM(S)
(Set out below the facts that form the legal basis for your other claim(s). Attach an additional page if you need more space.)

Put a line through any blank space left on this page

In a joint application for divorce, there will be two signatures — one for each spouse. But in an application where the applicant's only claim is for divorce, you and your lawyer are the only ones who will sign and you should strike out the inappropriate zone for your spouse's signature and corresponding date.

_____ _____
Signature of applicant husband *Date of signature*

_____ _____
Signature of applicant wife *Date of signature*

LAWYER'S CERTIFICATE

My name is:. . . . .
and I am the lawyer for (name) . . . . in this divorce case. I certify that I have
complied with the requirements of section 9 of the *Divorce Act*.

_____ _____
Lawyer's signature *Date of signature*

Q: A couple are separated but not divorced, and one spouse has signed a real estate listing agreement. What steps should be taken prior to formal divorce to ensure that the proceeds will be properly divided?

A: The real estate agent and the real estate lawyer should be told of the separation and keep all proceeds in trust until the parties can agree on their division.

It used to be that, if you worked for the federal government, your income would be exempt from seizure by a spouse. Many people used to change jobs from the private sector to the public sector after a divorce in order to avoid the seizure of assets enforcing support orders. Governments are now concerned about spouses who default, and legislation exists to track parties and ensure that support payments are made — regardless of employer.

Q: How does equalization work under the Family Law Act?

A: **Equalization** is the process of adjusting assets between spouses. A list is made, and whoever has more must, in most cases, pay money to the other spouse. There are exemptions for things such as inheritances that one party may have received.

Q: When splitting assets in a divorce, what is the 50% equalization based on? Is it the original purchase price of an item or the current value?

A: Generally, assets are valued as of the date of divorce.

**FROM THE ONTARIO COURT OF APPEAL
IN THE CASE OF LAY vs. LAY
MARCH 29, 2000**

FROM THE JUDGMENT OF ABELLA J.A.:

1   **ABELLA J.A.:** — The parties entered into a marriage contract on May 24, 1995, the day before their marriage. Under the terms of that contract, the wife was to retain sole ownership of certain property "free from any claims by the husband." Thirteen years later, the wife, as petitioner in a divorce proceeding, brought a motion under Rule 21 of the Rules of Civil Procedure for an order to determine an issue before trial. That issue was the validity of the marriage contract and, in particular, whether it exempted the property from the equalization provisions in the Family Law Act, R S.O. 1990, c. F.3.

13 In the contract before us, property was defined as the wife's shares and capital in two corporations. The parties agreed in paragraph 4 of the contract that the wife would retain sole ownership of this property "free from any claim by the husband." In my view, this unambiguous provision, along with paragraph 5 of the contract, make the parties' intentions irrefutably clear and satisfy the requirements in s. 70(3) of the Family Law Act.

14 Under paragraph 5 "all rights and obligations" of the husband and wife in connection with the possession, ownership, or division of the designated property are to be governed by the terms of the

agreement. The agreement is to prevail over "all provisions of the Family Law Reform Act (Ontario) or any successor", necessarily including ss. 4 and 8.

16 The essence of this contract is that the defined property was to be the wife's alone for all purposes, regardless of any provisions of the Family Law Reform Act or any successor legislation. The husband contracted out of any claim to a share in this property. It is difficult to see how the parties could have made their intentions clearer that the property was to be exempt from any otherwise applicable matrimonial property regimes, including the one set out under ss. 4 and 8 of the Family Law Reform Act.

17 I would, therefore, allow the appeal with costs throughout, set aside the order of Speigel J., and declare that the marriage contract dated May 24, 1995, is valid and binding, and exempts the designated property from the application of the equalization calculations in s. 5 of the Family Law Act.

Support

Q: **Are my Old Age Security and Canada Pension Plan payments seizable by my creditors?**

A: In the case of *Metro Toronto v. O'Brien*, the Ontario Superior Court had to deal with that very issue. The city had provided certain services to O'Brien and sued him for payment. It obtained judgment and attempted to seize his bank account. The CIBC objected to the seizure, arguing that the money represented OAS and CPP benefits.

The parties went to court, and the court agreed that the money was unseizable since it was protected by a law meant to provide each Canadian with a basic level of support.

Q: How does one enforce an order for support?

A: Courts recognize the need for support. They will assist parties by ordering disclosure of assets. Simply put, each side draws up a list of income, expenses, and assets. There is then an adjustment so that each spouse ends up with the same amount. Depending on these figures, one spouse may have to pay the other support or money to equalize the bottom line. If one spouse fails to disclose income or assets, then he or she can be ordered by a court to disclose. If one spouse fails to pay support, then he or she will be brought to court to justify the refusal to pay. If there is no justification, then the court will order that payment be made. If the order is not respected, then the court can order the seizure of assets and income by means of a court sheriff, who will do the legwork to seize them.

Q: How does one enforce support orders in other provinces?

A: There is a system of enforcement countrywide, and courts recognize orders given in sister provinces.

Q: Can long-term support be changed given a change in economic circumstances?

A: A change in support depends on the divorce agreement reached between the parties. If there is a clause indicating that no further adjustments will be made, then generally nothing further can be done (although recent rulings may allow spouses to reopen separation agreements). If no such clause exists, then a court can consider varying the amount of support paid.

> The Supreme Court of Canada recently considered the case of a high-profile lawyer who was economically better off than his ex-spouse. The court ruled that this was unfair and adjusted the previous agreement between the parties. The case took years to resolve. Courts are reluctant to overturn agreements freely made or court orders made with lawyers' input. Yet, if the circumstances are clearly unfavourable to one side or the other, then they will intervene.

Q: Is there an obligation to pay support to a 17-year-old who no longer lives with a parent?

A: Once a child is no longer dependent, the support for that child can stop. Another factor to consider is whether that child is in school and in need of support for his or her education. A dependant is someone who is in the care of another both financially and emotionally. The law will limit the time for support if the child is a professional student in his or her mid-20s.

Custody

Q: How does one go about obtaining joint custody of a three-month-old child?

A: A lawyer will file papers with a court seeking joint custody. A judge will then consider joint custody of the child. Factors such as income, home life, and emotional support will be considered. Independent psychological assessments of the parents may be required for the court to properly assess the child's situation.

Q: One spouse obtained custody of a child and then wondered whether the other spouse could challenge that arrangement.

A: If there are no changes in circumstances, and the child has not complained about the home environment, then there is no reason why custody should change. Custody usually changes when there is a major change in circumstances, when one of the ex-spouses has been informed of a complaint, or when the child is unhappy in his or her home environment. Nothing stops a challenge being brought, though it may not be successful.

Q: Is an ex-spouse with higher income obligated to pay for the children's education?

A: In general, when spouses separate, there is an equalization of assets between them. If one spouse is less able to afford a child's education, then the appropriate support adjustment may be made. Therefore, if one spouse makes more money than the other, then he or she may be forced to contribute toward the children's education.

Q: One member of a separated couple wishes to appoint a guardian in the event of death. How should she do this?

A: When she prepares a will, she can provide for the guardianship of her children. If there are no other documents dealing with this issue, then her will can set the rules for guardianship. If, on the other hand, a separation agreement has been prepared, then it may provide for guardianship or custody in the event that she dies before the children come of age.

Q: My boyfriend left me three years ago while I was pregnant. He is the father but has never seen the child, and I have never received child support. Does he have a claim on the child?

A: As the father, he has the right to see the child unless a court order is obtained barring access. A court will consider the father's lack of interest in the child's upbringing in making its decision. The court may also consider the financial and emotional support given by the mother and, if adequate, may well bar access by the father.

Disciplining Children

Section 43 of the Criminal Code states that "Every school-teacher, parent or person standing in the place of a parent is justified in using force by way of correction towards a pupil or child, as the case may be, who is under his care, if the force does not exceed what is reasonable under the circumstances." The Canadian Charter of Rights and Freedoms provides, in

Section 7, that "Everyone has the right to life, liberty and security of the person and the right not to be deprived thereof except in accordance with the principles of fundamental justice." Section 12 of the charter further provides that "Everyone has the right not to be subjected to any cruel and unusual treatment or punishment."

Thus, the Criminal Code allows for parents or schoolteachers to physically discipline children. The charter provides some protection. The issue currently before an Ontario court is whether the section of the Criminal Code is unconstitutional in light of the charter.

A 1999 Angus Reid poll indicated that only 16% of Canadians believed that spanking children should be a criminal offence. Ultimately, this issue will be resolved as the case winds its way to the Supreme Court of Canada.

Separation

Q: A couple were married for seven years and had four children prior to separation. It has now been several years since the separation, and they would like to obtain a divorce. There are no assets to settle and no support payments to make, and the parties are on relatively good terms. How can they obtain a divorce in the most cost-effective way?

A: The first thing that they should do is draft an agreement saying that all the property items are settled and that there are no further support obligations from one to the other. This document can be drawn up directly between them or through a lawyer. The next step is to obtain divorce papers through a legal stationer or the court. The details of the marriage and separation have to be clearly spelled out in these documents. Once completed, they are filed with the court, and a fee is paid to the Ministry of Finance. If the clerk accepts the documents as complete, then he or she will notify the ex-spouses within a few weeks that their divorce has been granted. Alternatively, the parties can see a lawyer on the basis of an uncontested divorce, and the lawyer will prepare all the necessary papers and advise them once the divorce has been granted.

Q: On what grounds can a separation agreement be reviewed? The lawyers for the spouses disagree on the interpretation of certain clauses.

A: A separation agreement can be reviewed by a third party, a lawyer, a mediator, or the court if the agreement itself does not prevent any form of review.

FROM THE ONTARIO COURT OF APPEAL
IN THE CASE OF DEROON vs. DEROON
SEPTEMBER 16, 1980

FROM THE JUDGMENT OF LACOURCIERE J.A.:

Generally speaking, *at common law*, a separation agreement could only be set aside if it was shown to have been entered into under duress or as a result of undue influence, fraud, or material misrepresentation or other unconscionable conduct. Lack of independent legal advice was considered to be an important factor.

The governing principle at common law, and the effect of the decisions in this Province and other common law Provinces in Canada, was correctly and accurately stated in a commentary written by Professor Bradley E. Crawford in 44 *Can. Bar Rev.* 142 (1966) at p. 143, and adopted as an "accurate statement of the law" by Schroeder, J.A., delivering the judgment of the Court in *Mundinger v. Mundinger*, [1969] 1 O.R. 606 at p. 610, 3 D.L.R. (3d) 338 at p. 342:

> *"If the bargain is fair the fact that the parties were not equally vigilant of their interest is immaterial. Likewise if one was not preyed upon by the other, an improvident or even grossly inadequate consideration is no ground upon which to set aside a contract freely entered into. It is the combination of inequality and improvidence which alone may invoke this jurisdiction. Then the onus is placed upon the party seeking to uphold the contract to show that his conduct throughout was scrupulously considerate of the other's interests."*

Q: Can an ex-spouse find out if her former spouse has remarried or is receiving other forms of income that would affect support payments?

A: Short of hiring a private investigator, it is hard to determine an ex-spouse's new financial circumstances. If the information is obtained, however, then support payments can be reviewed and perhaps cancelled. This is subject to the original separation agreement itself, which may prevent review of support payments for a set period of time. The agreement may also require ongoing financial disclosure, which is recommended, or it may be court ordered.

Q: A couple were married in Quebec and later moved to Ontario. In Quebec, by law, women are entitled to keep their maiden names. Since they now live in Ontario, does she have to use her married name, or can she keep her maiden name?

A: There is no requirement in Ontario that she use her married name, so she can continue to use her maiden name. In Quebec, a woman can do the same, although on official certificates she can use her maiden name, her married name, or a hyphenated combination of them.

Marriage Contracts

When you marry in Quebec, you can draft a marriage contract dealing with each spouse's property. This contract will set out what each spouse owned prior to marriage and how marital property is to be owned. If you don't have a contract, the law will specify who owns what.

In Ontario, you needn't have a contract, and the law only specifies a 50/50 division when you separate from your spouse.

After the PQ election in 1976, many Quebeckers moved to Ontario. They took with them their possessions and certain legal baggage such as their marriage contracts. Most couples haven't realized the full impact of these contracts.

For example, some contracts provide for a large gift from husband to wife to prevent creditors from taking away all the matrimonial property. If a couple divorce in Ontario, can that gift be enforced? The answer is probably yes, since Ontario law allows married couples to have contracts governing their property.

Thousands of ex-Quebeckers haven't realized that their Quebec contracts can be enforced in Ontario.

**FROM THE ONTARIO COURT OF APPEAL
IN THE CASE OF VIEN vs. VIEN
FEBRUARY 3, 1988**

FROM THE JUDGMENT OF LACOURCIERE J.A.:

I. *The facts*

Donat Vien married Anita Leclerc in the Province of Quebec on August 10, 1935. At the time of the marriage, the husband was aged 28 and his wife was 22. Some four days before the marriage, they had signed a marriage contract, prepared by a notary in Hull, Quebec, whereby, the future spouses agreed to become separate as to property, the future husband agreeing to provide, by way of gifts, real and personal property to the value of $3,000 within a period of five years.

. . .

Devos v. Devos, and other cases, support the statement found in Castel, *Conflict of Laws*, 3rd ed. (1974) at p. 237:

> *Where there is an express marriage contract or settlement, a change of domicile does not affect the rights of the spouses with respect to property acquired before or after the change of domicile. Actually domicile does not appear to be a relevant connecting factor. The proper law of the contract applies.*

. . .

On the basis of the expert evidence, and having concluded

that the Quebec law governed the spouses' property rights, I agree that the claim based on the common law doctrine of constructive trust and unjust enrichment could not succeed under Quebec civil law and that the action was properly dismissed.

. . .

IV. *The common law cause of action*

In view of the trial judge's conclusion, with which I agree, that the proper law of the contract is the civil law of the Province of Quebec, it is unnecessary to consider whether the evidence would have supported a recourse on the basis of the common law doctrines applicable in Ontario.

Q: An individual's parents were separated in the early 1990s after 25 years of marriage. There was a certain amount of animosity since the individual's father met, dated, and moved in with another woman. Some years later, the father died. He had been receiving old-age pension benefits from the government. Both the individual's natural mother and the unmarried spouse claimed these pension benefits. The government eventually split the pension between both "spouses." Is this proper?

A: Yes. The federal government on application can divide a pension between married and common-law spouses. The former spouse would also have a claim against her ex-husband's estate should there be any sums available under it.

Q: A couple were separating, and the husband wondered whether he could place an ad in the newspaper stating that he would no longer be responsible for his wife's debts. Is this proper?

A: An ad is not required but is often used to notify all creditors that one spouse is no longer responsible for the other's debts. Should anyone later state that he or she is responsible, the ad could be used as evidence in a lawsuit. The best thing, however, is to notify all known credit card companies that the spouses have separated and that one is no longer responsible for the other's debts. A separation agreement could also cover credit card and like debts. The agreement could also contain clauses protecting one spouse from lawsuits; in the event of a lawsuit, one spouse would be required to compensate the other.

Sample Marriage Contract

THIS IS A MARRIAGE CONTRACT made on _____ day of _____, 2001.

BETWEEN:

AND:

____(Name)____	("Spouse 1")
____(Name)____	("Spouse 2")

INTERPRETATION

1. In this contract,
   a) *"Spouse 1"* means _(Name)_, who is a party to this contract;
   b) *"Spouse 2"* means _(Name)_, who is a party to this contract;
   c) "Family Law Act" means the Family Law Act of Ontario, 1986;
   d) "property" and "net family property" mean property or net family property as defined in Part I of the Family Law Act;
   e) "family residence" means the buildings and lot located at _(Address)_ in _(City)_, Ontario, but does not include any other buildings or lot acquired in substitution for them;
   f) "breakdown of the marriage" means
      i) the separation of the parties with no reasonable prospect that they will resume cohabitation;
      ii) the dissolution of their marriage; or
      iii) the annulment of their marriage.

2. An act of the legislature or Parliament referred to by name will mean that act in force at the material time and includes any amendment or any successor act that replaces it.

BACKGROUND

3. The following items set out some of the background information to this contract.
   a) *Spouse 1* is employed by _____.
   b) *Spouse 2* is employed by _____.
   c) *Spouse 1* and *Spouse 2* have cohabited from time to time during a period of approximately (#) years preceding the making of this contract.
   d) *Spouse 1* and *Spouse 2* intend to marry each other on (Date).
   e) They intend to live in the family residence.
   f) The family residence is owned by (Name) and has a mortgage in favour of (Financial Institution).

PURPOSE OF CONTRACT

4. Each party intends by this contract
   a) to avoid any rights and obligations relating to any property that arise or that may in the future arise at law or in equity from their marriage;
   b) except as specifically provided by this contract, to elect and affirm that none of the property of either party will be divided between them except according to ownership; and
   c) if there is a breakdown of the marriage, to make specific provision for the division after the breakdown of any increase in value of the family residence accruing between the effective date of this contract and the date of the breakdown of the marriage.

AGREEMENT

5. Each party agrees with the other to be bound by the provisions of this contract.

EFFECTIVE DATE OF CONTRACT

6. This contract takes effect on the date the parties marry.

DOMESTIC CONTRACT

7. This is a marriage contract entered into under Section 52 of the Family Law Act and is a domestic contract that prevails over the same matters dealt with in the act.

FINANCIAL PROVISION

8. The responsibility for making financial provision for the family during cohabitation under the marriage will be assumed jointly by the parties in proportion to their respective financial abilities as may be agreed upon from time to time.

SUPPORT AFTER BREAKDOWN OF MARRIAGE

9. If there is a breakdown of the marriage, each party will have such rights to receive financial support from the other and will be under such obligations to provide financial support to the other as are given or imposed upon each party by the Family Law Act or the Divorce Act.

NO NET FAMILY PROPERTY

10. Under no circumstances will any property owned by either party, or by them together, be included in the net family property of either party.

RIGHTS OF OWNERSHIP GOVERN PROPERTY DIVISION

11. Each party waives all rights under Part I of the Family Law Act, and in lieu thereof each with the other provides by this agreement that
   a) rights of ownership govern the division of property between them, and there shall be no division of property except according to ownership;
   b) neither of them will be entitled to property rights arising out of their marital relationship;
   c) neither of them will be entitled to a division of property owned by the other;
   d) neither of them will be entitled to the equalization of their net family properties; and
   e) neither of them will be entitled to a share of any property or the value of any property owned by the other,
notwithstanding
   f) they are cohabiting;
   g) they are married;
   h) one party is improvidently depleting or may improvidently deplete his or her net family property;
   i) they are separated;
   j) a divorce is being, or has been, granted;
   k) the marriage is being, or has been, declared a nullity; or
   l) one party has died leaving the other surviving.

WAIVER AND RELEASE

12. Each party
   a) waives all rights and entitlement, and
   b) releases and discharges the other and his or her estate from all claims that he or she has on the effective date of this contract or

may later acquire under the Family Law Act or under the laws of any jurisdiction;

c) to a division of property or the value of property owned by the other,

d) to the equalization of their net family properties or other sharing of their net family property, and

e) to any property or value of property owned by the other,

on any basis notwithstanding

f) they are cohabiting;

g) they are married;

h) one party is improvidently or may improvidently deplete his or her net family property;

i) they are separated;

j) a divorce is being, or has been, granted;

k) the marriage is being, or has been, declared a nullity; or

l) one party has died leaving the other surviving.

DEEMED OWNERSHIP

13. Subject to an appropriate instrument in writing, the rule of law applying a presumption of resulting trust shall not apply in questions of ownership of property between the parties, and

a) property transferred from one party to the other party shall be deemed to be owned by the party to whom the property is transferred;

b) property held in the name of one party shall be deemed to be owned by that party;

c) property held in the name of both parties as joint tenants shall be deemed to be owned by both parties as joint tenants; and

d) money on deposit in the name of both parties shall be deemed to be in the name of the parties as joint tenants.

NO OWNERSHIP UNLESS LEGAL OWNERSHIP

14. Except as provided by this contract, each party
    a) waives all rights and entitlement, and
    b) releases and discharges the other and his or her estate from all claims that he or she has on the effective date of this contract or may later acquire;
    c) in equity by way of constructive, implied, or resulting trust, or by way of any other doctrine in equity, and
    d) at law under the Family Law Act and the laws of any jurisdiction,
to
    e) compensation; and
    f) any interest in property or the value of property owned by the other,
by reason of
    g) the transfer of property to the other without any or any adequate payment or other consideration;
    h) work, money, or monies worth contributed to the acquisition, management, maintenance, operation, or improvement of property, or
    i) any other fact or circumstance creating a beneficial interest in property.

RIGHT TO DEAL WITH SEPARATE PROPERTY

15. Except in the case of the family residence, each party may dispose of or encumber or otherwise deal with his or her property as he or she deems fit, free from any claim by the other, as if he or she were unmarried.

FAMILY RESIDENCE

16. Each party acknowledges that
    a) The family residence is owned by (Name), and each agrees with the other that it will remain his/her separate property.
    b) If there is a breakdown of the marriage, (Name) will pay (Name) a sum equal to one half of any increase in the market value of the family residence accruing between the effective date of this agreement and the date of the breakdown of the marriage as determined under the next section of this agreement.
    c) The sum will be payable within 30 days after the amount is determined.
    d) The right of (Name) to share in the increase in value is an ownership interest in the family residence to the extent of the value realized by the right.

INCREASE IN MARKET VALUE

17. The increase in market value of the family residence will be the increase accruing between
    a) the effective date of this contract, and
    b) the date of the breakdown of the marriage.

18. The market value on the effective date of this contract is $(Value).

19. The market value on the date of the breakdown of the marriage will be the value determined by
    a) the agreement of the parties; or
    b) the opinion of a single qualified appraiser selected by both parties; or
    c) the agreement of a qualified appraiser selected by (Name) and a qualified appraiser selected by (Name);

d) if the two appraisers selected in (c) cannot agree, by the opinion of a third qualified appraiser selected by the two appraisers.

20. If within 30 days from the date of the breakdown of the marriage
   a) the market value of the date of the breakdown has not been determined; and
   b) arrangements have not been made to pay _(Name)_ a sum equal to one half of any increase in the market value;
   either party may apply under the Family Law Act for sale of the family residence.

21. Any order for sale made under the Family Law Act must provide for
   a) a reference to the master to determine the interests of the parties as set out in this contract;
   b) the right of each party to purchase the interest of the other; and
   c) such other directions as may be necessary for the expeditious realization of the respective interests of the parties.

RIGHTS RELATING TO MATRIMONIAL HOME

22. Nothing in this contract restricts or modifies the rights of either party with respect to the possession, disposition, or encumbrance of the family residence (which each party acknowledges to be a matrimonial home under the Family Law Act) or any other matrimonial home as defined under the Family Law Act, but each of the parties intends that if there is a breakdown of the marriage, _(Name)_ will give _(Name)_ vacant possession of the family residence as of the date of the breakdown, although he or she is not and cannot be bound by this contract to do so.

CONTENTS OF FAMILY RESIDENCE

23. If there is a breakdown of the marriage of the parties, the contents of the family residence or any successor residence will be distributed between the parties according to ownership whether that ownership arises by way of purchase or gift, including gifts from the other party.

RELEASE AGAINST BUSINESS INTERESTS

24. Without restricting the generality of the other waivers and releases in this contract, and subject to transfers or bequests that may be made, each party
   a) waives all rights, and
   b) releases and discharges the other and his or her estate from all claims that he or she has or may in the future acquire under the laws of any jurisdiction, and particularly under the Family Law Act and the Succession Law Reform Act, entitling him or her upon the death of the other
      i) to a division of property owned by the other or to one half the difference between their net family properties or to any other share of this difference, or to any share of the property of the other;
      ii) if the other party dies leaving a will, to elect against taking under the will in favour of receiving an entitlement equalizing their net family properties, or in favour of any other benefit;
      iii) if the other party dies intestate, to elect to receive an entitlement in intestacy or to receive an entitlement equalizing their net family property;
      iv) if the other party dies testate as to some property and intestate as to the other property, to elect to take under the will and to

receive an entitlement in intestacy, or to receive an entitlement equalizing their net family properties;

v) to share in the estate of the other under a distribution in intestacy in any manner whatsoever;

vi) to receive support as a dependant from the estate of the other in any manner whatsoever; and

vii) to act as executor and administrator of the estate of the other.

TRANSFER OR BEQUEST OF PROPERTY TO OTHER PARTY

25. Either party may, by appropriate written instrument,

a) convey or transfer during his or her lifetime, and

b) devise or bequeath for distribution after his or her death,

any property to the other, or appoint the other as executor of his or her estate. Nothing in this contract will limit or restrict in any way the right to receive any such conveyance, transfer, devise, or bequeath from the other, or, if so appointed, the right to act as executor or administrator of the estate of the other.

FINANCIAL DISCLOSURE

26. Each party

a) has fully and completely disclosed to the other the nature, extent, and probable value of all his or her significant assets and all his or her significant debts or other liabilities existing at the date of this contract and, in addition to this disclosure,

b) has given all information and particulars about his or her assets and liabilities that have been requested by the other,

c) is satisfied with the information and particulars received from the other, and

d) acknowledges that there are no requests for further information or particulars that have not been met to his or her complete satisfaction.

AMENDMENT OF CONTRACT

27. Any amendment of this contract will be unenforceable unless made in writing and signed by each party before a witness.

GOVERNING LAW

28. This contract will be governed by the law of the Province of Ontario.

SEVERABILITY

29. The invalidity or unenforceability of any provision of this contract will not affect the validity or unenforceability of any other provision, and any invalid provision will be severable from this contract.

CONTRACT TO SURVIVE DIVORCE

30. If a divorce is granted, or if the marriage is declared a nullity, the terms of the contract will survive the event and continue in force.

CONTRACT TO SURVIVE DEATH

31. This contract is intended to survive the death of a party or parties and will be binding on the heirs, administrators, executors, and assigns of the deceased party or parties.

INDEPENDENT LEGAL ADVICE

32. Each party acknowledges that he or she
    a) has had independent legal advice;
    b) understands the nature and the consequence of this contract; and
    c) is signing this contract voluntarily.

TO EVIDENCE THEIR AGREEMENT, each of the parties has signed this contract under seal before a witness.

SIGNED, SEALED, AND DELIVERED

_____   _____

Witness as to the signature of   Spouse 1

_____   _____

Witness as to the signature of   Spouse 2

FOR SPOUSE 1
CERTIFICATE AND AFFIDAVIT OF EXECUTION

I, (Name), of the City of (Place), in the Province of (Place), MAKE OATH AND SAY AS FOLLOWS:

1. I am the solicitor for (Name), and a subscribing witness to this contract, and I was present and saw it executed at the City of (Place), by the said (Name).

2. I believe that the person whose signature I witnessed is the party of the same name referred to in the contract.

3. I have advised the said (Name) with respect to the within contract, and I believe that he is fully aware of the nature and consequences of the contract on and in light of his present and future circumstances and is signing it voluntarily.

SWORN before me
at the City of _____, in the
Province of _____,
this ____ day of _____
200_.   _____
                                                                (Signature)

A Commissioner etc.

FOR SPOUSE 2
CERTIFICATE AND AFFIDAVIT OF EXECUTION

I, (Name), of the City of (Place), in the Province of (Place), MAKE OATH AND SAY AS FOLLOWS:

1. I am the solicitor for (Name), and a subscribing witness to this contract, and I was present and saw it executed at the City of (Place), by the said (Name).

2. I believe that the person whose signature I witnessed is the party of the same name referred to in the contract.

3. I have advised the said (Name) with respect to the within contract, and I believe that she is fully aware of the nature and consequences of the contract on and in light of her present and future circumstances and is signing it voluntarily.

SWORN before me
at the City of _____, in the
Province of _____,
this ____ day of _____
200_.   _____
                                                            (Signature)

A Commissioner etc.

CHAPTER THREE

Company Rights

There is a well-known soap opera known as "The Young and the Restless." The title aptly describes some company employees who are young and wish to set out on their own. They have ideas, they are restless, and they believe that they could benefit by forming their own companies.

While many fail, many succeed. The vehicle they use is known as a company or corporation. These are interchangeable terms. A company is nothing more than an alter ego of the founding members with some neat legal benefits.

To set up a company, you have to file incorporation papers with either the federal or the provincial authorities. You must list who are the founding members and pay a prescribed fee. The government will then either confirm the name that you have suggested or give you a number such as 12345 Canada Inc. This is your company.

Your lawyer will then prepare a set of rules and regulations for the company. These are called the by-laws. They are akin to the constitution of a country as the company sets out the rights and obligations of each member. Should you choose not to use a lawyer, many stationery stores sell incorporation kits with some standard wording for these by-laws.

Once you have set out your by-laws, the next step is to open a bank account. The bank will require additional signed documentation, and you will then have cheques printed with the company name on them.

Next you will have to apply for tax numbers. The government will issue you numbers for income taxes, payroll deductions, and GST.

Armed with the by-laws, cheques, and government tax numbers, you are now ready to do business.

There are benefits to setting up a company. The first is that a company pays less tax than an individual does. Whereas, in some cases, the marginal tax rate is 50%, corporations pay roughly half of the personal amount. This is meant to encourage people to set up businesses, since the business will not only pay tax but also employ individuals, who in turn will pay taxes. They will also stimulate the economy.

The second major benefit of a company is that it does not die. It continues well after you have retired and moved on. In the event that the company does not do as well as you expected, it can file for bankruptcy. Unless you have personally guaranteed certain loans for the company, or personally guaranteed certain supplies, your liability is limited to your investment. If your company goes bankrupt, then you lose your investment. Hence, limited liability is an attractive feature for people setting up companies.

These benefits are meant to encourage you to try something new, since, if it works, everyone benefits.

Following are some basic questions and answers in the area of company rights.

Ownership

Q: How do I show that I own a company?

A: Ownership of a company is indicated in the form of a document called a **share certificate**. It shows that you have an interest in the company. If you have a majority of all shares issued by that company, then you control it.

Q: What types of shares can companies issue?

A: There are two basic types of shares issued by a company. The first is a **common share**, and the second is a **preferred share**. Both types entitle the holder to receive dividends, which are another form of profit distribution. They may even provide for no dividends. However, the preferred shares rank ahead of the common shares. Therefore, if you own only preferred shares, then you will receive the first cut of any money in the company. If there is not enough money to go around, and you own only common shares, then you will receive nothing.

Q: Can I pass on my shares to my heirs?

A: Yes. A share in a company is like any other piece of property, and it can be passed on to your next of kin.

Q: Can I incorporate a company on my own?

A: There are incorporation kits available, and the forms are straightforward. The proposed company name will have to be cleared with the appropriate federal or provincial companies directorate. You can do it on your own, but if you have partners it's best to have all your documents checked by a lawyer to make sure everything is in order. The money you spend will be worth it if only to avoid future problems.

SAMPLE COMMON SHARE

SAMPLE INCORPORATION DOCUMENT I

▌◆▌	Consumer and Corporate Affairs Canada	Consommation et Affaires commerciales Canada	
	Canada Business Corporations Act	Loi régissant les sociétés par actions de régime fédéral	**FORM 1** ARTICLES OF INCORPORATION (SECTION 6)	**FORMULE 1** STATUTS CONSTITUTIFS (ARTICLE 6)

1 — Name of corporation   Dénomination de la société

2 — The place in Canada where the registered office is to be situated   Lieu au Canada où doit être situé le siège social

3 — The classes and any maximum number of shares that the corporation is authorized to issue   Catégories et tout nombre maximal d'actions que la société est autorisée à émettre

4 — Restrictions, if any, on share transfers   Restrictions sur le transfert des actions, s'il y a lieu

5 — Number (or minimum and maximum number) of directors   Nombre (ou nombre minimal et maximal) d'administrateurs

6 — Restrictions, if any, on business the corporation may carry on   Limites imposées à l'activité commerciale de la société, s'il y a lieu

7 — Other provisions, if any   Autres dispositions, s'il y a lieu

8 — Incorporators — Fondateurs

Name(s) — Nom(s)	Address (include postal code) Adresse (inclure le code postal)	Signature

FOR DEPARTMENTAL USE ONLY — À L'USAGE DU MINISTÈRE SEULEMENT Corporation No. — N° de la société	Filed — Déposée

7530-21-936-1385 (01-93) 46

SAMPLE INCORPORATION DOCUMENT II

▮✦▮ Consumer and Corporate Affairs Canada	Consommation et Affaires commerciales Canada	**FORM 3** NOTICE OF REGISTERED OFFICE OR NOTICE OF CHANGE	**FORMULE 3** AVIS DE DÉSIGNATION OU DE CHANGEMENT
Canada Business Corporations Act	Loi régissant les sociétés par actions de régime fédéral	OF REGISTERED OFFICE (SECTION 19)	DU SIÈGE SOCIAL (ARTICLE 19)

1 — Name of corporation – Dénomination de la société

2 — Corporation No. — N° de la société

3 — Place in Canada where the registered office is situated   Lieu au Canada où est situé le siège social

4 — Address of registered office   Adresse du siège social

CAUTION: Address of registered office must be within place specified in articles, otherwise an amendment is required (Form 4) in addition to this form
AVIS : L'adresse du siège social doit se situer à l'intérieur des limites du lieu indiqué dans les statuts. Sinon, une modification est requise (formule 4)

5 — Effective date of change   Date d'entrée en vigueur du changement

6 — Previous address of registered office   Adresse précédente du siège social

Date	Signature	Title – Titre
7530-21-936-1386 (01-93) 46		Filed – Déposée

SAMPLE INCORPORATION DOCUMENT III

◼◼◼	Consumer and Corporate Affairs Canada	Consommation et Affaires commerciales Canada	FORM 6 NOTICE OF DIRECTORS OR NOTICE OF CHANGE	FORMULE 6 LISTE DES ADMINISTRATEURS OU AVIS DE CHANGEMENT
	Canada Business Corporations Act	Loi régissant les sociétés par actions de régime fédéral	OF DIRECTORS (SECTIONS 106 and 113)	DES ADMINISTRATEURS (ARTICLES 106 et 113)

1 – Name of corporation – Dénomination de la société	2 – Corporation No. – N° de la société

3 – The following persons became directors of this corporation   Les personnes suivantes sont devenues administrateurs de la présente société

Name Nom	Effective date Date d'entrée en vigueur :	Residential address – Adresse domiciliaire	Occupation	Resident Canadian – Y/N Résident canadien – O/N

4 – The following persons ceased to be directors of this corporation   Les personnes suivantes ont cessé d'être administrateurs de la présente société

Name Nom	Effective date Date d'entrée en vigueur :	Residential address – Adresse domiciliaire

5 – The directors of this corporation now are   Les administrateurs de la présente société sont maintenant

Name – Nom	Residential address – Adresse domiciliaire	Occupation	Resident Canadian – Y/N Résident canadien – O/N

Date	Signature	Title – Titre

7530-21-936-1388 (01-93) 46

Field – Déposée

Partnerships

Q: How is a partnership different from a company?

A: A company has limited liability. The liability of individuals who own the company is restricted to the amount they invest and the shares they own. A partnership, on the other hand, involves two or more people working together, and each is personally responsible for the full amount of the debts incurred by the partnership. There is also a risk in a partnership in that individual assets such as your home can be seized to satisfy partnership debts.

Q: Can a company own property?

A: A company can own property, just as an individual can own property. The company can own not only real hard assets, such as land and equipment, but also what is known as intellectual property. **Intellectual property**, simply put, is the thinking of a person's mind that evolves into a design and ultimate product. The company can own the rights to this product and the efforts of people working for the company.

Hiding Assets

Individuals and companies that face a lot of debt may consult a credit counsellor, a lawyer, or an accountant. They in turn would advise their clients about possible means of restructuring their debts and, if necessary, filing for bankruptcy. Bankruptcy allows an individual to cancel his or her debts and return to society as a productive member. Companies in bankruptcy can be wound up. Individuals and companies have been known to squirrel away assets in the hope that creditors will not find them and use them to pay off debts.

This concept of transferring assets is not new. The first known case occurred in 1601 and is known by law students as "Twyne's case." Mr. Twyne had sheep and feared that his creditors would seize his sheep. He approached a neighbour and suggested that he transfer the sheep to his neighbour but, as the case reports, "keep them and use them for his own purposes." Creditors were somehow alerted to this transfer and went to court to challenge it. The creditors were successful, and the sheep were sheared and sold. The farmer's debts were paid.

The principle of transfer of property in order to fraudulently defeat creditors was subsequently enshrined in law and is known by the name of the monarch who ruled at the time, Elizabeth I. The statute is called the **Statute of Elizabeth**.

Public and Private Companies

Q: What is the difference between a public and a private company?

A: A private company is owned by a finite group of people, whereas a public company is listed on a stock exchange. Shares in this public company are traded regularly and can be bought and sold subject only to the number of shares issued by the company and traded on the stock market.

Q: Can shares of a company be held by a trust?

A: Yes. Shares can be owned either by an individual or by a trust. A trust is a separate legal entity whereby one person administers the property for another.

Liability

Q: Are companies responsible or liable to customers if something goes wrong?

A: A company is no different from a person in the event that something goes wrong. If a person causes damage, then he or she can be held liable for it. If a company causes damage, then it can be sued and also held liable.

Manufacturers' Liability

Every law student will learn of the case of the snail in the bottle. A poor resident of England drank some ginger beer only to find a snail at the bottom of the bottle. She sued the manufacturer for pain and suffering and was ultimately successful. The case set the benchmark for manufacturer's liability. Many years have passed since the case was decided, and students have studied the law surrounding that case and all similar subsequent cases.

Recently, the estate papers of the aggrieved person were reviewed. The heirs discovered a note indicating that the man had placed the snail in the bottle after drinking a few sips.

Notwithstanding this intentional act, the principle still remains, and a manufacture (along the chain of supply from from provider to manufacturer) is still responsible to provide a safe and healthy product. However, damages in Canada in this type of situation are not as great as those in the United States or England.

Canadian cases have included a person who ate chocolate-chip cookies only to discover that the chocolate chips were mouse droppings and a person who found a small animal inside a cereal box. In Canada, damages for this type of injury range from $2,000 to $7,000. Not a lot of money when you consider what a person might have ingested.

Financing a Business

Small businesses face many challenges, one of which is to get adequate financing. A 1988 study (which has yet to be updated) by the Canadian Federation of Independent Businesses had this to say:

Banker turnover appears to have a direct, negative impact on small business financing.

As turnover increases, the likelihood that a financing application will be turned down or cut back increases; the average rate charged on loans increases; the amount of collateral required to support the loan increases; and the rate of small business dissatisfaction with the loan and the borrowing experience increases. There is no single bank factor that appears to have such a direct and negative impact on the terms and conditions under which small business borrows than high banker turnover. Once again, the level of banker familiarity with the business and its owner comes to the fore as a key determinant of the availability of small business financing under reasonable terms and conditions. The implication is that identical businesses facing different levels of banker turnover may receive differential treatment by the chartered banks. The problem is that banker turnover is not controllable by small business.

Table 2.14 shows the aggregate levels of banker turnover faced by small businesses in this study.

Table 2.14

**Number of Account Managers
You've Had at Current Bank in Last 3 Years**

	Percent	
One	24.0	
Two	33.2	
Three	19.3	
Four	5.6	27.6
Five or more	2.7	
No answer	15.2	
	100.0	

Disputes

Q: What can I do if I have a dispute with a company or other shareholders?

A: If you own shares in a public company, then you can sell them. If you own shares in a private company, then you can try to have the company purchase them from you in an effort to withdraw from the business. If the company refuses to purchase your shares, then there are mechanisms under company law that will allow you to have your shares evaluated by an independent third party, and the company can be forced to purchase them at that value.

In the event of a dispute between members of a company, the law provides a mechanism called **the oppression remedy**. A person who feels "oppressed" by the company can apply to a court, which can do a number of things. The court can regulate the affairs of the company, remove officers, or adequately compensate you for your interest in the company.

Courts have sometimes been quite creative in helping shareholders to evaluate their shares. They can order independent appraisals, have the property sold to a third party, or force one of the parties to purchase the other's interest.

**CANADIAN BUSINESS CORPORATIONS ACT
EXCERPTS FROM THE SECTION
ON THE "OPPRESSION REMEDY"**

234. (1) **Application to court re oppression.** — A complainant may apply to a court for an order under this section.

(2) **Grounds.** — If, upon an application under subsection (1), the court is satisfied that in respect of a corporation or any of its affiliates

(a) any act or omission of the corporation or any of its affiliates effects a result,

(b) the business or affairs of the corporation or any of its affiliates are or have been carried on or conducted in a manner, or

(c)   the powers of the directors of the corporation or any of its affiliates are or have been exercised in a manner that is oppressive or unfairly prejudicial to or that unfairly disregards the interests of any security holder, creditor, director or officer, the court may make an order to rectify the matters complained of.

(3) **Powers of court.** — In connection with an application under this section, the court may make any interim or final order it thinks fit including, without limiting the generality of the foregoing,

(a)   an order restraining the conduct complained of;

(b)   an order appointing a receiver or receiver-manager;

(c)   an order to regulate a corporation's affairs by amending the articles or by-laws or creating or amending a unanimous shareholder agreement;

(d)   an order directing an issue or exchange of securities;

(e)   an order appointing directors in place of or in addition to all or any of the directors then in office;

[Para. (e) substituted by 1978-79, c. 9, s. 74.]

(f)   an order directing a corporation, subject to subsection (6), or any other person, to purchase securities of a security holder;

(g)   an order directing a corporation, subject to subsection (6), or any other person, to pay to a security holder any part of the moneys paid by him for securities;

(h)   an order varying or setting aside a transaction or contract to which a corporation is a party and compensating the corporation or any other party to the transaction or contract;

(i)   an order requiring a corporation, within a time specified by the court, to produce to the court or an interested person financial statements in the form required by section 149

or an accounting in such other form as the court may
determine;

(j)   an order compensating an aggrieved person;

(k)   an order directing rectification of the registers or other
records of a corporation under section 236;

(l)   an order liquidating and dissolving the corporation;

(m)   an order directing an investigation under Part XVIII to be
made;

(n)   an order requiring the trial of any issue.

**FROM THE ONTARIO SUPERIOR COURT
IN THE CASE OF WITTLIN vs. BERGMAN
JULY 8, 1994**

FROM THE JUDGMENT OF FARLEY J.:

Law is to be the representative of the applicants and Bergman
the representative of himself and Inc. They are to jointly and
equally fund the preparation of the following physical arrangement. The determination contemplated is to take place forthwith.
At the head office of Cookies (or such other place as mutually
agreed), there is to be a buzzer which may be operated by one
of two buttons. There is to be an arrangement whereby if one button is pushed, there is an acknowledgement of which button has
been so pushed and an override to prevent the other from registering. A stop-watch will be placed so that each can see the dial.
Only the faces of Law and Bergman are to be seen by the other.

Thus there should be no way for the other one to determine or detect that one will be pushing the buzzer until it is pushed (except to the extent of guessing as to what the facial reactions mean or do not mean). The stop-watch is to be activated. Each six seconds the price will drop from $527,272 based on a 20 per cent share interest (if Bergman and Inc. are bought out the price will be four times that) so that after one minute the price will be reduced to $517,272 (and so on). When the buzzer is pushed the stop-watch is to be halted. The elapsed time will determine the purchasing price for 20 per cent (or four times that in the case of the applicants buying). For example if X pushes the buzzer after three minutes and 36 seconds, the preliminary price will be $491,272. Then Y (the non-pusher) shall have the opportunity of "electing to kick or receive". That is the non-pusher Y shall have the option of requiring that X buys Y's shares or alternatively that X sells X's shares to Y, at the preliminary price (as adjusted for four times in the event of Bergman's and Inc.'s shares). (i) If Y offers his shares for X to buy them X may elect to purchase Y's shares for the preliminary price. However, if X does not wish to buy Y's shares, then X in turn may require Y to buy X's shares at 80 per cent of the preliminary price. (ii) If Y elects to buy X's shares, then Y may do so for the preliminary price. A valid decision to buy the other side's shares ends the process.

For clarity, if X ends up the buyer of Y's shares, then Y does not buy X's shares and vice versa. The reference to X's shares and Y's shares means 100 per cent of the shares of Cookies (i.e., X and Y are to be authorized to deal with all the shares of each respective side's shares). The preliminary price to start out for the shares of the applicants shall be $527,272 and in the case of Bergman and Inc. four times that (or $2,109,088).

POSTSCRIPT — July 8, 1994

The question was raised after the release of my handwritten reasons as to the discipline effected by such a mechanism given that the person who first pushes the button can ultimately require the other to purchase his shares at a 10 per cent discount from the preliminary price. I have adjusted for this by requiring as set out above a 20 per cent discount as I think there is merit in having a more significant differential to maintain the necessary discipline. However, it also seems to me that the discipline to be truly exercised here is as to which side truly wishes to obtain ownership of Cookies, all within a general price range which both sides thought was in the ball park a year ago and there does not appear to have been a collapse of the operations since then. Clearly the certainty obtained by this process and the elimination of the fighting would seem to be positive features for the future fortunes of Cookies.

Order accordingly

(*The case was subsequently overturned on appeal)

Q: **To form a business partnership in Quebec, should the parties use a notary or a lawyer?**

A: In Quebec, the legal profession has two branches. The first is comprised of notaries, who primarily take care of drafting legal documents. The second is comprised of lawyers, who generally are licensed to go to court. To form a business partnership, contracts will have to be drafted, and it is preferable that a notary undertake that exercise.

If the law had to define a "thumb," then it would use the format of the Income Tax Act and start with the concept that you don't have a thumb and then decree that you do have one. Let me illustrate.

The Thumbs Act

Section 1:
A person has no thumbs on one hand.

Section 2:
Notwithstanding Section (1), where a person other than a company or partnership has hands, and is about to compute the number of thumbs at a particular time, on a particular hand, the following rules apply.

(a) Determine the aggregate of objects each of which is a hand, and from that aggregate, if any, subtract an amount equal to that aggregate less one.

(b) In respect to the number of hands determined in paragraph (a) above, determine the aggregate of digits, if any, attached to that hand immediately before that time.

(c) From the aggregate determined in paragraph (b) above, deduct an amount that is not greater or less than the number of appendages, if any.

(d) For the purposes of paragraph (c) above, appendages means fingers.

Patent and Trademark

Q: An engineer has developed a new element in aircraft design. How does she apply for a patent?

A: Patent law is one of the most complex areas of the law, and patent lawyers often hold engineering or science degrees as well as law degrees. They ensure that no one has a similar concept registered with the government. A patent is recognition from the government that your idea is unique and that you and only you are entitled to exploit it. If your product is unique, then a patent will be issued. If you obtain a patent through some error, and a patent has already been registered, then any profits you make may have to be repaid to the original patent holder. Patent lawyers spend a lot of time analysing various patents to ensure that the new one is indeed unique. Because of the time spent on research, and since lawyers bill by the time they spend on a file, applying for a patent becomes very expensive.

Patents can be obtained at several levels. You can get a Canadian patent for under $10,000 in legal fees. U.S. patents are more expensive since they are often recognized in other countries even though they haven't been registered there. A U.S. patent carries prestige, just as in the high-tech sector the "dot.coms" carry more prestige.

A worldwide patent is even more expensive since your lawyer will have your patent verified through various regulatory levels in various countries. The best recommendation is to start small and obtain a Canadian patent. If the concept takes off, then you will have enough money from it to register your product worldwide.

Canadian Directors

Did you know that, in order to incorporate a Canadian company, a majority of directors must be Canadian? Although the Foreign Investment Review Act has been abolished in Canada, we still have laws that protect people starting up Canadian companies.

Q: **If person A owns a registered trademark, and person B owns a domain name on the World Wide Web with the same name, can the domain name be transferred to person A?**

A: A domain name is a registered name identifying your particular mailing address and web site. If you own a preregistered trademark in a name, then you and only you are entitled to use the same domain name. If someone else has registered that domain name, he or she can be forced to give it up to you as well as any profits made by using it. The whole area of domain names is evolving, and international conventions are being drafted to avoid this type of dispute.

Trademarks and the Internet

The Canadian Trade Marks Act prohibits the registration of common names. So, for example, you cannot register "socks" or "shoelaces" or "pants" as a trademark. This rule does not apply, however, when it comes to the Internet. As long as no one else has registered the same name, you can register "pants" followed by

".com." Internet entrepreneurs have registered every conceivable verb, adverb, noun, and adjective, hoping to strike it rich. So, if a major computer company wanted to use "computer.com," it may not be able to since it is already registered and owned by someone else.

This conflict between trademarks and Internet name registrations has led to many lawsuits between the owner of a trademark and the company that registered the Internet name. Slowly, all governments will get involved in regulating this activity. For example, the government of the United States has appointed the Internet Corporation for Assigned Names and Numbers (ICANN), an agency that is to try to manage and regulate the naming system. The Canadian Internet Registration Authority (CIRA) has attempted to set up a dispute-resolution system so that the various companies and individuals owning trademarks and names can sort out their disputes without lengthy court battles.

Whereas company law has been around for a while, Internet law is new and evolving. The law will have to be as creative as the innovators behind new domain names.

Trusts

Q: A wife recently separated from her husband. He owned a retail store, and she was the named trustee for the company that owned the store. She is now worried about her liability for actions taken by the company during her time as trustee, given that the parties are now separated. She was not involved in day-to-day matters since her ex-husband did most of the management. What are her liabilities?

A: In most cases, there is a trust document setting out the rights and obligations of the parties. If there is no written agreement, then the following basic principles apply.

1. A trust is a separate legal entity whereby one person holds property for another.

2. A trustee is liable first to the beneficiary for breach of the rules governing the trust and second to any person harmed by the actions of the trust.

In this case, the ex-husband cannot complain of actions since he took day-to-day management of the business affairs. If there has been fraud in terms of diverting money from Revenue Canada, then that agency will no doubt sue the trust and the trustee; if sued, the trustee can sue the beneficiary (ex-husband) for compensation, all in the same lawsuit.

The parties should work out their respective rights and obligations so that there are no further disputes should a lawsuit be brought.

Miscellaneous Matters

Sex and the Law

The courts and the media have recently focused on sex in the workplace or between co-workers. In a recent case, two police officers were caught having sex on videotape, which surveillance was meant to catch an equipment thief. Two executives on an overseas flight were charged for nuisance since they had sex while in their assigned seats.

Courts in New Brunswick and Ontario have heard cases of estranged spouses suing their significant others' employers for not preventing office affairs. They argued that the employers should have had set standards and discouraged the affairs from starting in the first place.

An employer must provide a safe work environment, and that includes an environment that does not encourage interoffice sex. Aggrieved family members could sue if the employer knew that sex was taking place and did nothing to stop it. Workers' safety in all forms must be paramount when an employer sets up shop and hires employees.

Q: Can I sue my ex-wife's boss for having had an affair with her?

A: Subject to proving that the events took place and subject to workplace policies and safeguards, recent cases suggest that you can sue. Your "compensation" would be monetary damages, and that is often the difficult issue. What amount would adequately compensate you for what has occurred? It's not an easy question, and the courts have yet to set those guidelines. I would suggest that it may be the cost of your subsequent divorce, associated support obligations, if any, and compensation for mental anguish. Estimated total: $50,000.

Landlords

When a company fails to pay its rent, the landlord can, in most circumstances, close down the business and seize assets located there. Sometimes the landlord will have competing interests. Certain suppliers of equipment or supplies may have first claims against some assets. A dispute may arise between the landlord and the secured creditors about who owns what. When a secured party has retained ownership of the equipment or goods, the landlord must pay for them before seizing and selling them. If there is no reserved ownership, then it is a question of who can seize the items first.

Recent cases have dealt with certain fixtures that have been attached to the landlord's premises by the company/tenant. In some cases, these pieces of equipment are large and require that they be firmly installed on or in the building. This type of equipment, landlords have argued, then forms part of the over all structure, so the landlord should retain priority over it. The Ontario Court of Appeal recently ruled that these fixtures, even though they are attached, do not form part of the landlord's property.

In all cases, it is wise to have the lease spell out who owns what and who can seize what. When you enter into agreements with suppliers of equipment or goods, be sure to spell out who has the right to seize the items in the event of a default in payment.

Q: How do I prevent disputes from arising with my business partner?

A: First, your company by-laws must be clear and provide a mechanism for voting. Second, you should have a shareholders agreement setting out what to do in the event of a dispute and how to evaluate each partner's respective interests. Spell it all out as in a marriage contract so that, when things are working out, you can provide for when they aren't.

Sample Shareholders Agreement

executed in the City of _____, Province of Ontario,
as of this ____ day of _____, 200_.

BY AND BETWEEN:

SHAREHOLDER #1

of the City of _____, Province of _____
(hereinafter referred to as "#1"),

-and-

SHAREHOLDER #2

of the City of _____, Province of _____
(hereinafter referred to as "#2"),

-and-

SHAREHOLDER #3

of the City of _____, Province of _____
(hereinafter referred to as "#3"),

-and-

123456789 CANADA INC.

(hereinafter referred to as "the company")

WHEREAS the company was incorporated under the Canada Business Corporations Act (the "Act") by Articles of Incorporation dated the ____ day of _____, 200_.

AND WHEREAS the authorized share capital of the company consists of an unlimited number of common shares of which the following are issued and outstanding as fully paid and non-assessable:

Shareholder #1	10 common shares
Shareholder #2	10 common shares
Shareholder #3	10 common shares

AND WHEREAS the parties hereto desire to provide for their mutual protection, if any one of them dies or wishes to withdraw from the corporation.

NOW THEREFORE IN CONSIDERATION OF THE MUTUAL COVENANTS HEREINAFTER CONTAINED, THE PARTIES HERETO AGREE AS FOLLOWS:

ARTICLE I
PREAMBLE

1.1   The preamble hereto shall form part hereof as if herein recited at length.

ARTICLE 11
UNANIMOUS SHAREHOLDERS AGREEMENT

2.1   Notwithstanding any provision of this agreement to the contrary, the powers of the director(s) of the company to manage the business and affairs of the company, whether such powers arise from the charter, the by-laws of the company, or otherwise, are hereby fully restricted to the extent permitted with respect to the matters set forth herein.

ARTICLE III
BOARD OF DIRECTORS

3.1 That for so long as the present agreement remains in effect, the board of directors shall be restricted to

Shareholder #1
Shareholder #2
Shareholder #3

or their nominees or representatives.

3.2 That the parties hereto shall vote at all meetings of the shareholders and take all steps as may be necessary to ensure the director(s) is/are elected or appointed and maintained in office as members of the board of directors as provided for under paragraph 3.1 hereof.

ARTICLE IV
OFFICERS

4.1 The officers of the company shall be as follows:

Shareholder #1	**President**
Shareholder #2	**Vice President**
Shareholder #3	**Secretary-Treasurer**

4.2   The officers of the company shall not incur any personal liability as a result of the execution of their functions hereunder, towards the parties or towards any third party, and the parties hereto shall hold harmless the others against any and all claims, actions, or other proceedings that may be brought against them resulting from the execution of their functions provided thereunder, unless such claims result from their gross negligence, fraud, unauthorized acts, or other neglect of fiduciary duties.

ARTICLE V
TRANSFER OR DISPOSAL OF SHARES

5.1   Except as provided herein, the parties hereto shall not sell, transfer, assign, or otherwise dispose of their shares, nor shall they mortgage, hypothecate, pledge, or charge in any manner any of their shares except with the unanimous consent in writing of the other shareholders.

5.2   Subject to the provisions hereof, the parties hereto agree and undertake not to sell, transfer, assign, or otherwise dispose of their shares to any third party unless such third party will accept in writing to be bound by the provisions of and become a party to this shareholders agreement.

ARTICLE VI
AUTHORIZED TRANSFERS

6.1   Notwithstanding the provisions of any article herein, a party hereto may transfer his shares held in the share capital of the company to a company incorporated and controlled by such shareholder (the "holding company"), the said transfer to occur without the consent of the other shareholders, provided that the holding company will accept in writing to be bound by the provisions of and become a party to this shareholders agreement and that the transfer of share restrictions contained herein shall apply to any transfer of shares of the holding company.

6.2 For the purposes of this agreement, the expression "shareholder" or "party" shall include the shareholders, signatory parties hereto, as well as any holding company to which such shareholder's shares shall have been transferred.

ARTICLE VII
CALL OPTION

7.1 Each of the shareholders (hereinafter referred to as the "purchasers") shall have the right (hereinafter called the "call option") exercisable at any time upon the resolution of the shareholders of the company adopted by all remaining shareholders who are the holders of at least 66% of all the issued and outstanding voting shares of the company at a shareholders' meeting duly convened for the purpose thereof to require any other shareholder (hereinafter referred to as the "seller") to sell to the purchasers all, but not less than all, of the shares in the capital of the corporation beneficially owned by the seller (hereinafter referred to as the "seller's shares").

7.2 The call option shall be exercised by the purchasers giving to the seller notice in writing (hereinafter referred to as the "Notice to Exercise") of their intention to exercise the call option.

7.3 Upon exercise of the call option, the seller shall be obligated to sell to the purchasers, and the purchasers shall be obligated to purchase, the seller's shares in accordance with the provisions of Section 7.4 hereof, and on a pro rata proportionate basis according to the shareholders at the time of the purchaser. In the event that any one or more purchasers are unwilling to purchase a portion of the seller's shares herein, then the remaining purchasers shall have the right to acquire and purchase on a pro rata basis those shares that the unwilling shareholder would have otherwise been entitled pursuant to this section.

7.4   The sale and purchase of the seller's shares under Section 3 hereof shall be completed on the following terms and conditions.

a) The purchase price payable for the seller's shares shall be the fair market value thereof as at the date on which the Notice of Exercise is given to the seller, as determined by the auditors of the company in accordance with such generally accepted valuation procedures as such auditors consider appropriate in the circumstances.

b) In the event of a dispute as to the auditors' valuation, either party may refer the issue to arbitration in accordance with clause 15.1 of this agreement. The shareholders agree to cause such auditors to (a) make such determination within three days following the giving of a Notice of Exercise; and (b) to report on such determination, including all details of all elements and factors taken into consideration in making such determination, in writing to each of the shareholders;

c) The purchase price so determined shall be paid to the seller in full at the time of completion of the transaction;

d) The seller's shares shall be free and clear of any liens, mortgages, charges, and encumbrances whatsoever, and the seller shall have good and marketable title thereto;

e) Upon the completion of the transaction, the seller will, and will cause his nominee(s) to, resign from all offices and positions with the corporation;

f) The completion of the transaction shall take place at 11:00 a.m. local time on the first business day following the date, being 30 days after the date on which the auditors of the corporation have reported under sub-section 7.4(a) hereof; and

g) The purchasers shall cause the seller to be fully released from all obligations under any guarantees or indemnities that have been given by the seller for or in respect of any debts, liabilities, or obligations of the corporation.

7.5 In the event that the federal and/or provincial authorities determine that the selling price of the shares were undervalued, the purchasers shall pay to the seller an amount equal to the tax liability, including interest and penalties, demanded by the governmental authorities.

7.6 For the purpose of this clause, the liability and obligation of the purchasers to the seller shall be joint and several.

ARTICLE VIII
BANKRUPTCY, INSOLVENCY OPTION

8.1   Each of the shareholders hereby grants to the other of them an irrevocable option (the "option"), which option shall be exercisable only upon the bankruptcy, insolvency winding up, or liquidation of the granting shareholder, or in the event that a receiver is appointed in respect of the whole or substantially the whole of such shareholder's property and assets (any such trustee, receiver, or transferee being hereinafter called the "special transferee"), and the said shareholder (being hereinafter called the "insolvent shareholder").

8.2   The other shareholders (being hereinafter called the "solvent shareholders") shall have the right to purchase the insolvent shareholder's shares in the capital of the corporation at a purchase price determined by the auditor valuation provision contained in Article VII of this agreement.

ARTICLE IX
RIGHT OF FIRST REFUSAL

9.1   If any shareholder (hereinafter referred to as the "seller") desires and intends to sell all or any part of the shares of any class of shares in the capital of the company beneficially owned by the seller (hereinafter referred to as the "subject shares"), the seller shall give to the other shareholders (hereinafter referred to as the "offerees") notice in writing (the "offer") offering to sell the subject shares to the offerees or any one or more of them on a pro rata proportionate basis in accordance with their share holdings at the time that offer shall specify the price per share and the terms and conditions on which the seller desires to sell the subject shares.

9.2   Upon the offer having been given to the offerees in the manner provided above, the offerees or any one or more of them shall have 10 banking days from the date of receipt of such offer within which to accept the offer by giving the seller notice in writing (hereinafter referred to as an "acceptance") that the offerees agree to purchase the subject shares referred to in the offer, on the terms and conditions and at the price per share specified in the offer, subject to the provisions of this section. If the offerees fail to refuse to give an acceptance within the time prescribed, they shall be deemed to have refused to accept the offer.

9.3   If the offerees give an acceptance to the seller within the time prescribed, the offerees shall purchase all of the subject shares on a pro rata basis in accordance with their respective proportionate share holdings at the time at purchase price and on the terms and conditions set out in the offer.

9.4   If the offerees fail or refuse to give an acceptance to the seller within the time prescribed, the seller may then offer the subject shares for sale to any one or more persons, firms, or corporations dealing at arm's length (within the meaning of the Income Tax Act) with the shareholders, provided that the seller may offer only the subject shares and that the subject shares may only be offered at a price per share not less than the price per share stipulated in the offer and on terms and conditions not more favourable to a purchaser than the terms and conditions stipulated in the offer.

ARTICLE X
PRE-EMPTIVE RIGHTS

10.1 The parties hereto agree that no shares of any class of shares in the capital of the company shall be allotted or issued to any shareholder or third-party subscriber therefor (the "subscriber") unless such shares (the "additional shares") have first been offered to all shareholders for purchase by them on a pro rata basis in proportion to their then existing holdings of common shares and at the same subscription price per share as the additional shares are proposed to be offered to the subscriber by the corporation.

10.2 Such offer shall be made in writing by the corporation, and each shareholder shall then have 10 days from receipt of such offer within which to accept such offer for all, but not less than all, of such shareholders' pro rata share of the additional shares, by delivering to the corporation a written subscription and tendering payment in full of the subscription price of such shares.

10.3 Any shareholder who fails to accept the offer within the said 10-day period in the manner provided aforesaid shall be deemed to have refused to subscribe for and purchase his pro rata share of the additional shares so offered hereunder.

ARTICLE XI
CONVERSION

11.1 Upon the death of a shareholder, the estate of the deceased shareholder shall have the right, exercisable on 10 days' written notice to the company, to convert all, and not less than all, of the deceased's common shares in the company into special shares on the basis of one special share for each common share so converted, failing notice of exercise the provisions of Article XII shall apply.

11.2 The special shares shall be non-voting and non-participating.

11.3 Upon conversion, the share certificates for the special shares resulting therefrom shall be issued in the name of the estate of the deceased shareholder or as it might otherwise direct and be dealt with as an asset of the estate of the deceased shareholder, provided that such new registered holder shall pay any applicable security transfer taxes or any other taxes that may apply.

ARTICLE XII
SALE OF SHARES ON DEATH OF A SHAREHOLDER

12.1 Subject to the provisions of Article XI and provided the estate of a deceased shareholder does not elect to convert the shares of the deceased shareholder pursuant to that article, upon and within 90 days of the death of a shareholder, the survivors shall purchase and the estate of the deceased shareholder shall sell the shares now owned or hereafter acquired by the shareholder who is first to die. The purchase price shall be the value as provided for in the auditor valuation provisions in Article XII of this agreement. A surviving shareholder shall purchase that portion of the shares owned by the deceased represented by the ratio of the number of shares owned by such survivor to those owned by all the survivors.

12.2 If no executor or administrator is appointed for the estate of a deceased shareholder within 90 days after his death, the surviving shareholders shall be considered creditors of the estate of the deceased party with all the rights conferred upon a creditor of the estate of the decedent by the place of his domicile, including the right to cause an executor or administrator to be appointed. If any party becomes missing, such party shall be conclusively presumed dead after he has been missing for 12 consecutive months.

ARTICLE XIII
SHARE CERTIFICATE ENDORSEMENT

13.1 Each certificate evidencing ownership of shares shall have endorsed upon it a statement to the following effect: "The shares evidenced by this certificate are subject to restrictions on their transfer and their voting rights and to the provisions of a unanimous shareholders' agreement and are transferable in accordance with the provisions of the said agreement."

ARTICLE XIV
INTERVENTION

14.1 The company intervenes hereto to take knowledge of the terms and conditions set forth herein and to ensure in the event of a sale, assignment, transfer, or other conveyance by any party hereto, of any or all of their shares, in a manner contrary to the terms hereof, that no such transfer shall be made or shall be effective and that such transfer not be recorded in the books of the company until the proposed transferee has intervened in this agreement and becomes bound hereby or has been deemed to have been intervened.

ARTICLE XV
ARBITRATION

15.1 All matters in dispute under this agreement shall be referred to arbitration, the award and determination of which shall be final and binding upon the parties hereto, the whole in accordance with the provisions of the Arbitration Act.

ARTICLE XVI
TERMINATION

16.1 This agreement has an indefinite term, subject to earlier termination in the event of

a) the liquidation, dissolution, winding up, or other termination of the corporate existence of the company;

b) an agreement in writing of all of the shareholders; or

c) all of the voting shares being owned by a single shareholder.

16.2 This agreement ceases to be binding on a shareholder when he has fully disposed of all of his shares.

ARTICLE XVII
CONFLICT WITH BY-LAWS AND ARTICLES

17.1 If this agreement conflicts with the articles or by-laws, the provisions of this agreement shall govern. Each shareholder shall vote or cause to be voted the shares owned by him as necessary so as to cause the articles or by-laws or both, as the case may be, to be amended to resolve any such conflict in favour of the provisions of this agreement.

ARTICLE XVIII
GOOD FAITH

18.1 The principle of the utmost good faith shall govern the parties, in all their relations as shareholders, directors, and officers.

ARTICLE XIX
AMENDMENT OF AGREEMENT

19.1 This agreement may be altered, amended, or annulled at any time during the lives of the shareholders hereto by the mutual and unanimous consent in writing of all the parties hereto.

ARTICLE XX
FUTURE SHARES

20.1 This agreement shall relate to the shares of the company now owned by the shareholders as set forth in this agreement and to such additional shares of the company as may hereafter be acquired by any one or more of them.

ARTICLE XXI
FUTURE ACTIONS

21.1 The parties shall do all acts and things and execute all documents that may be reasonably necessary or advantageous to enforce this agreement according to its tenor and intent.

ARTICLE XXII
TIME

22.1 Time shall be in every respect of the essence in this agreement.

ARTICLE XXIII
COUNTERPARTS

23.1 This agreement may be executed in any number of counterparts, each of which shall be deemed in original but all of which shall constitute one agreement.

ARTICLE XXIV
INTERPRETATION

24.1 It is the desire of the parties hereto that this agreement be accorded a liberal interpretation consistent with its declared intent and purposes and in accordance with the laws of the Province of Ontario.

24.2 The headings appearing throughout this agreement are inserted for convenience only and form no part of this agreement. Should any portion of this agreement be declared invalid by a court of competent jurisdiction, the elimination of such portion shall not affect the remainder of the agreement, which shall remain in full force and effect.

ARTICLE XXV
INDEPENDENT LEGAL ADVICE

25.1 The parties hereto each acknowledge that

a) each has been advised and urged to obtain independent legal advice and has had independent legal advice or the opportunity of obtaining such advice;

b) has read the agreement in its entirety and has full knowledge of the contents;

c) understands his or her respective rights and obligations under this agreement, the nature of this agreement, and the consequences of this agreement;

d) is entering into this agreement without any undue influence, fraud, duress, or coercion whatsoever; and

e) is signing this agreement voluntarily.

IN WITNESS WHEREOF this agreement has been executed by the parties hereto at the place and as of the date first hereinabove mentioned.

_____

Shareholder #1

_____

Shareholder #2

_____

Shareholder #3

123456789 Canada Inc.

Per:_____

I have authority to bind the corporation.

When companies do business, it is always prudent to have a contract setting out who is to do what and when. A company will specify the services or products to be provided, and the customer will confirm his or her obligation to pay for them.

When companies explore new business relationships, they may have to disclose some of their technological expertise or business methods. To ensure that they remain company property, many companies enter into a nondisclosure agreement to protect themselves from the loss of expertise. Samples of these agreements are on the following pages.

Sample General Contract

THIS AGREEMENT made this ___ day of _____, 200_,

BETWEEN:

_____

                    Hereinafter referred to as "the company"

AND:

_____

                    Hereinafter referred to as "the customer"

WHEREAS the company provides ___(services)___;

AND WHEREAS the customer wishes to engage the services of the company;

NOW THEREFORE THIS AGREEMENT WITNESSETH that in consideration of the mutual promises and covenants herein contained and for other good and valuable consideration, the receipt and sufficiency of which are hereby acknowledged, the parties agree as follows:

1. The company agrees to perform, and the customer agrees to engage, the services of the company in accordance with Schedule "A" attached, and the customer acknowledges that the services provided remain the intellectual and copyright property of the company.

2. The customer agrees to pay certain fees, and the company agrees to invoice in accordance with Schedule "B" attached, payable within 30 days of invoicing.

3. The customer agrees to provide the company with whatever facilities are required by the company to carry out this agreement.

4. The customer agrees on behalf of itself and its associates, employees, and agents that they will not contract, deal, or otherwise enter into any transactions with any other entity introduced to it by and through the efforts or contacts of the company without the express written consent of the company.

5. The terms of this agreement shall apply to any extensions of business accruing beyond that originally contemplated by this agreement and to any rollovers, follow-ups, repetitions, renegotiations, renewals, or subsequent transactions or contracts for the benefit of the parties, their administrators, successors, or assigns arising directly or indirectly as to the performance of their obligations under this agreement.

6. This agreement may be terminated by either party on six (6) months' written notice without forfeiting the amounts due for the period prior to the termination date.

7. In the event of a dispute between the parties, which they are unable to resolve between themselves, the matter shall be submitted exclusively to an arbitrator for determination in accordance with the Arbitration Act in force in the Province of Ontario, Canada.

8. This agreement shall be governed by and construed exclusively with the laws of the Province of Ontario, Canada.

9. This agreement shall not be assignable and has been duly authorized by corporate minutes with each party being deemed an independent contractor.

10. This agreement constitutes the entire agreement between the parties, and they acknowledge that there are no representations, agreements, understandings, or statements, oral or otherwise, express or implied, other than those expressly set forth in this agreement.

IN WITNESS WHEREOF, the parties have placed their hands and seals.

SIGNED IN THE   THE COMPANY
PRESENCE OF

_____   Per: _____

                           THE CUSTOMER

_____   Per: _____

SCHEDULE "A"

The parties agree on the following services being provided:

1. _____

2. _____

3. _____

4. _____

5. _____

SCHEDULE "B"

The parties agree on the following fee structure:

1. _____

2. _____

3. _____

4. _____

5. _____

Sample General Nondisclosure Agreement

THIS AGREEMENT is made on the ___ day of _____, 200_,

BETWEEN:

_____

(Hereinafter referred to as "the company")

AND:

_____

(Hereinafter referred to as "the customer")

WITNESSETH:

THAT WHEREAS the parties contemplate entering into, or participating in, one or more business transactions (hereafter individually and/or collectively referred to as "the subject business"); and

WHEREAS the parties mutually recognize that in the subject business each may learn from the other (including associates) the identities, addresses and/or telephone numbers of clients, agents, brokers, buyers, sellers, financiers, and/or bank or trust contacts (hereafter referred to as "confidential sources") and/or information relating to business plans, methods, concepts, and ideas (hereafter referred to as "confidential information") that the company has acquired by years of investment in time, expense, design, and effort;

NOW THEREFORE, in consideration of the mutual promises set forth herein, each party covenants and agrees with the other as follows:

1. That all confidential sources and confidential information of each
    party are valuable property and shall be and remain exclusive
    property of such party.

2. That neither party (including the associates, agents, affiliates, and/or
    representatives of such party) will attempt directly or indirectly to
    contact the other party's confidential sources or make any use of
    confidential information of the other party except through the
    parties to this agreement with the express written consent of the
    company as to each such contact and/or use. Any violation of this
    covenant shall be deemed to be an attempt to circumvent such
    other party, and the party so violating this covenant shall be liable
    for damages in favour of the party being circumvented.

3. Each party agrees that neither such party nor any associate, agent,
    affiliate, and/or representative of such party will disclose to any
    third person any confidential sources or confidential information.

4. Each party agrees with the other that upon any breach of this
    agreement the party in default will pay to the other party:

    a) the noncircumvention damages, if applicable, plus:

    b) all losses and/or damages sustained by the nondefaulting party
       by reason of such breach, plus:

    c) all expenses incurred in enforcing any legal remedy and/or
       right(s) based upon or arising out of this agreement, plus:

    d) all legal fees and disbursements incurred in relation to the
       breach.

5. In the event of dispute as to the meaning of enforcing this agreement, all parties agree to submit the matter to binding arbitration under applicable rules in the Province of Ontario, Canada.

6. The terms of this agreement apply and shall be binding upon rollovers, extensions, renewals, overages, parallel agreements, and/or transfers of contracts, their authorized representatives, affiliates, subsidiaries, agents, successors, heirs, or assigns introduced by one of the parties hereto to the other party.

7. This agreement shall be binding upon the parties, their heirs, successors, administrators, and assigns for a period of five (5) years from the date upon which the last signature has been affixed herein.

Date:_____   THE COMPANY

                           Per:_____
                           Signature

                           _____
                           Name/Title

Date:_____   THE CUSTOMER

                           Per:_____
                           Signature

                           _____
                           Name/Title

Conclusion

I hope that with this series of books, we have met the objective of providing basic information on questions that we all face when we come up against legal problems and issues. I hope that it will save you time and money when you need to consult a lawyer.

I also hope that you won't need to hire a lawyer, as it often means that you have a problem. Most matters can be resolved on your own by a letter or phone call. If not, then you *should* consult a lawyer, if only to clarify your rights. Then consider your options, as legal proceedings can be time consuming, emotionally draining, and costly.

For further information, your local courthouse will have pamphlets on basic rights, and the court staff is there to help you. Most government agencies are listed in the blue pages of your phone book. Courts and provincial law societies can be accessed on the World Wide Web. Use your favourite search engine and search for "court" or "law society" in your province. The Supreme Court of Canada has a web page located at www.scc-csc.gc.ca. Your local library will also have basic legal texts covering most areas of the law.

Thank you for using this book as a resource.

I hope that I have answered many of your legal questions. However, if your particular question needs to be answered or if there are follow-up issues that need to be addressed, you can write to me via the Internet by logging on to www.legalcounsel.ca.

Index